Sliding
into Home

Sliding into Home

A Memoir

KENDRA WILKINSON

with Jon Warech

G

GALLERY BOOKS

New York London Toronto Sydney

GALLERY BOOKS

A Division of Simon & Schuster, Inc.
1230 Avenue of the Americas
New York, NY 10020

First Gallery Books trade paperback edition October 2011

GALLERY BOOKS and colophon are trademarks of Simon & Schuster, Inc.

For information about special discounts for bulk purchases, please contact Simon & Schuster Special Sales at 1-866-506-1949 or business@simonandschuster.com.

The Simon & Schuster Speakers Bureau can bring authors to your live event. For more information or to book an event, contact the Simon & Schuster Speakers Bureau at 1-866-248-3049 or visit our website at www.simonspeakers.com.

Designed by Jaime Putorti

Manufactured in the United States of America

10 9 8 7 6 5 4 3 2 1

The Library of Congress has cataloged the hardcover edition as follows:

Wilkinson, Kendra.
    Sliding into home : a memoir / by Kendra Wilkinson ; with Jon Warech.
        p.   cm.
1. Wilkinson, Kendra.   2. Television personalities—United States—Biography.
3. Models (Persons)—United States—Biography.   I. Warech, Jon.   II. Title.
    PN1992.4.W547A3   2010
    791.450'28092—dc22
    [B]   2010017539

ISBN 978-1-4391-8091-4
ISBN 978-1-4391-8092-1 (pbk)
ISBN 978-1-4391-8093-8 (ebook)

To my son, Hank IV,
who marks the beginning of a
wonderful new chapter in my life.

Contents

CONTENTS

Introduction

*W*hen you star in a reality show, the entire world thinks they know you. Fans see you as the girl next door, tabloid editors see you as a story line, and paparazzi see you as a target. At the end of the day, they are all wrong.

Yes, I'm on TV, and yes, that makes me a celebrity, but I wake up every morning, look in the mirror, and see Kendra, a regular girl from humble beginnings who nowadays gets to do some pretty amazing shit. The girl you saw on *The Girls Next Door* and *Kendra* is only part of who I am. I really *am* a fun girl who likes to party, and I will kick some ass on a soccer or softball field, but I'm also a wife, a mother, a daughter, a friend, and so many other things to many different people.

Ultimately, I'm a real chick with real emotions, real concerns, and a growing sense of responsibility.

The crazy thing about television is that you are rarely allowed to grow. You are molded into a character based on some of your strongest traits and you are forced to stay that way for your entire television life. I was nineteen when *The Girls Next Door* started. All I cared about was having fun. If I'd written this book back then, it would be 250 pages about which tequila tastes better (Patrón) and when it's all right to flash your boobs (always).

In the past year and a half, my life has completely changed. I moved out of the Playboy Mansion, got married, and gave birth to my baby boy, Hank Jr. The way I look at life and fill my days now is as far from that nineteen-year-old as you can possibly imagine. I set a dinner table every night instead of dancing on one at a club. I wake up at five A.M. instead of passing out at that hour after a long night of partying. And if I'm whipping out a boob, it's probably because Hank Jr. is hungry.

But I wouldn't be the Kendra I am today without the life experiences I've had and, more important, the people who have been in my life throughout this entire journey.

Through all the good and bad, my mom has stuck by me. She didn't pick me up every time I fell; she let me get up on my own and learn from my mistakes, but was always there when I needed her. Hugh Hefner was the same way. He's the kindest, most thoughtful man on the planet, and he saw strength in me that I didn't even know existed. He let me fail and succeed on my own because he believed in me more than I believed in myself at the time. Holly and Bridget—there was probably a time when they wanted me to fail, but we all became good friends and learned to not judge a book by its cover. And Hank, well, he gave me his heart. True love changes a person. One day you care only about yourself, and then, before you know it, you are putting someone else first all the time.

It's because of them that I'm not the one-dimensional character you see on TV. Behind the laugh you hear on television, there is a girl who has been through some intense shit—stuff I'm proud of and stuff I'm not so proud of. But my life experiences shaped my personality and because of that experience I know I'll be a great mom. I needed to fail and succeed, to have loved and lost, and even to have shaken my ass on a dance floor to become a well-rounded, confident mother who won't freak out every time Hank Jr. starts to cry.

Without those experiences and the people who were along for the ride, who the hell knows where I'd be? I was always on the move as a kid, always getting into trouble, and I never had a clue where I would end up. My life was crazy, and it only got more insane when I packed up and moved into the Playboy Mansion. I was a wild child who could never sit still.

To this day, I still am all over the place. I moved from the Mansion to a condo in the Valley to Philadelphia to Indianapolis and back to L.A., all in the past year. I don't know where life will take me—I've always been a free spirit in that way—but I do know that with Hank and Hank Jr. by my side it doesn't matter where we live. As long as the three of us are together I will always feel like our house is a home . . . and that's the best feeling in the world.

CHAPTER 1

A Tale of Two Kendras

"So you'll be naked?"

"Well, I'll be painted," I corrected Zack, my live-in boyfriend.

"What does that mean?"

"I don't know, but I'm sure it will be fine."

I wasn't sure spending an evening as a painted girl at Hugh Hefner's seventy-eighth birthday party would actually be fine, but I was hoping it would turn out to be. At the very least, I would make a couple hundred dollars, meet some cool people, and get a chance to check out the Playboy Mansion. How could I turn that down?

And besides, it was Zack who had initiated the whole thing. He'd taken me to the car show where a photographer had said he wanted to set up a photo shoot with me, and at the time Zack was all for it. So it seemed totally logical that when the photographer posted the photos on One Model Place—a sort of MySpace for models—if any work came from it, Zack would support me.

Well, the photographer posted the photos, and that same day a guy named Mark called from *Playboy* and asked about me.

The truth is, I wasn't exactly sure what the Playboy Mansion was—or who Hugh Hefner was, for that matter. I knew about the bunny; I had an uncle who worked at the Playboy Club in Atlantic City, and he would send my brother and me T-shirts and sweatshirts with the bunny on them when we were kids. I'd wear them to school and all the kids would tease me and say *Playboy* was gross, but I thought it was cool.

Beyond that, I didn't know much about *Playboy*. But I knew enough to know that getting a phone call from someone who worked there could be the beginning of something big.

Mark's first call wasn't guaranteed to lead to anything. He mentioned that he was looking for girls to work at Hef's upcoming birthday party. I figured *Playboy* had a lot of models to choose from for the party, and it was a long shot. But a couple of days later Mark called back.

"Mr. Hefner saw a photo of you and wants to call you personally," he told me. "I gave him your number, so expect a call."

I was stunned. "What are you talking about? Expect a call? Why?" I was weirded out by the whole thing. Why would he want to call me?

"Listen," Mark said. "He only likes girls in college, so tell him you go to college."

I said okay and hung up, confused.

The next day I was in the shower when the phone rang. I hopped out and saw that the call was from a 310 number.

That's L.A. I was eighteen years old and lived in San Diego. Who did I know in L.A.?

"Hello?" I answered.

"Hello, is this Kendra?"

"Who is this?"

"This is Hugh Hefner."

"Yeah, right," I said, thinking it was a prank call. "Shut the fuck up."

It wasn't a prank.

"I look forward to seeing you at my birthday," he said. "Also, I'd like you to consider being my girlfriend."

Still dripping wet from the shower, I stood there in shock. I didn't know how to respond. After all, I had just told Hugh Hefner to shut the fuck up. That probably wasn't the reaction he'd expected. I brushed off the girlfriend thing, since I had no idea what that even meant. When I finally collected my thoughts, I told him I would see him at his birthday party.

Just as I was wrapping up the conversation, Zack walked into the bathroom to find out who I was talking to. After I filled him in, he was as shocked as I was, and clearly a little worried.

"I want to drive you up there," he said protectively.

When the big day arrived, I was kind of nervous. During the car ride Zack questioned me about how I was going to handle being invited to be Hef's girlfriend, but I didn't have an answer for him. Even though I googled Hef after we spoke on the phone, I couldn't really imagine what it might mean to be his girlfriend.

After a two-hour drive, Zack and I arrived at the gates of the Playboy Mansion in Bel Air. We buzzed security, who let us inside, and Zack pulled the car right up to the side entrance of the Mansion.

"Be good," he said as I opened the car door.

"Whatever," I mumbled back, barely even paying attention to him.

It was hard to focus once I got a good look at the Mansion. I was amazed at what I saw. Everything was so big and beautiful, and like nothing I had ever seen before. After all, I was a Hollywood virgin. Not *that* kind of virgin but, you know, still a little naive.

I got out of the car and was immediately escorted to the gym by security. I rushed by other girls and a handful of workers, and once inside the gym, Mark, who was the talent scout and body painter, told me to take off my clothes.

"Where's Hugh Hefner?" I asked as I stripped down.

"He never comes down here," Mark told me.

That sucks! I thought. I wanted to meet him and find out what he was all about.

Mark and his wife started painting me and putting rhinestones all over my body. It was all very weird. Then they moved away from my boobs and focused on my hair and makeup. I caught a glimpse of myself in the mirror. It was my first time ever having my hair and makeup done professionally, and I thought I looked like a drag queen.

Just as they were finishing making me a naked she-man, Hef—breaking his usual rule of staying out of the painted girls' room—came inside. He introduced himself and gave me a hug.

My heart was racing. "I've never met a celebrity before in my life," I said. "You are the first. This is the coolest thing."

It really was.

Hef laughed and we talked a little bit about the night. He told me not to be nervous and invited me to stop by his table. The conversation was short and sweet. He was very charming; he had a powerful way about him, and I liked it.

"I'll see you upstairs," he said with a smile before disappearing into the night.

For those few minutes with him I forgot that I looked like a clown. A naked clown. I felt special. After all, the staff probably went through thousands of photos to find about ten painted girls, and out of those ten, Hef singled me out. The man who had created this whole world chose *me*. That felt really good.

At the party I served Jell-O shots to celebrities like Jack Nicholson, Pauly Shore, Donovan McNabb, Fred Durst, and Brooke Burke. I was starstruck, but I didn't act like it. I simply went up to Brooke Burke, gave her a Jell-O shot, and politely told her that I loved her. I was cool like that.

The night ended up being a lot of fun. Being practically naked was not a big deal for me, and after a while I forgot that I didn't like my hair and makeup.

Then Mark came up to me and told me to bring some Jell-O shots to Hef's table.

"Are you sure?" I asked nervously after glancing at Hef's table, which was packed with beautiful women.

As I inched my way toward the group, Hef and I locked eyes. I smiled. He was with his girlfriends, including Holly and Bridget—who I didn't know at the time—and a bunch of Barbie look-alikes, but he kept looking at me. I offered them shots and hung around the table the rest of the night. Maybe I was paranoid, but I thought the girls were giving me dirty looks the whole time, and with my eyes I tried to tell them *I ain't trying to steal your man*, but I wasn't quite sure if the message was received.

The whole evening, Hef and I kept staring at each other. It wasn't a physical attraction for me, but he was just so cool. The way he acted and the things he said were unlike anything I had seen or heard before.

At the end of the night Hef came up to me, gave me a key, and asked me to stay the night. I couldn't—mainly because Zack was sitting outside the Mansion in his car, but beyond that, I felt that being there that night was a job, and I wanted to keep it that way. Clock in. Clock out.

I gave him the key back but told him I would see him again soon.

"Will you be my girlfriend?" he asked again before I left.

Staring into his eyes, I didn't see a man four times my age with ten times more girlfriends than most. Even though I hardly knew him yet, I saw a sweet man who made me feel really good about myself—a true gentleman. It was weird but in my heart, I felt like he was someone I could possibly trust.

"So, will you?"

There was only one thing I could say: "Um, okay."

⎯⎯⎯⎯

*T*hat night my life changed. I had no idea what I was getting myself into, but something just felt right about it. Hef didn't offer me money or tell me he was going to make me a star. He didn't say anything, because truthfully that wasn't the deal. He wasn't trying to offer me anything other than him (and maybe a pretty cool home).

I liked what I saw at the Mansion and, more important, I liked what I saw in Hef. He was a good guy with good intentions, and in a short period of time I was able to understand that about him, so I was willing to take a risk and uproot my entire life.

I don't know if many girls would do that on a whim. Such an offer would scare some girls, and others might look at Hef and see dollar signs and jump at the chance to do whatever he said. I didn't care about that at all. Looking into Hef's eyes I knew there was nothing to fear, and mansion or no mansion, I was drawn to him in a way that I had never been drawn to a man before.

I couldn't put my finger on it, but something about that night felt so right. A new life was definitely beginning, and I was not going to stop it from happening.

As you probably know, I became Hef's girlfriend, moved into the Mansion full-time, and a year later began filming the hit show *The Girls Next Door*.

I was labeled the sporty party girl of the bunch, and while I didn't like being labeled, I certainly had a good time living up to the character the producers wanted me to play.

Life has really worked out for me. Maybe it was luck or maybe fate, but I'm pretty blessed to be in the situation I'm in today.

While the show may have opened the door to a charmed life and eventually helped me discover what I really wanted, the

reality is, it didn't come easy. I wasn't just sitting around deciding which family business to take over when I got that call from
Hef. I didn't just trade in one perfect life for another. It's been
an uphill battle, and while life is great—almost perfect, even—
right now, before I can talk about the best of times, I need to tell
you about the worst . . .

CHAPTER 2

No Room for Daddy

I was three years old the first time my dad left us. We were living in Clairemont, a community in San Diego, California. I don't remember much from back then, so as far as I know there wasn't tons of fighting or anger within our house. But my dad wanted out.

My mom, Patti, says that my dad and I were really close when I was a baby. He would take me to the beach and spend lots of time with me. Then, when my mom got pregnant with my younger brother, Colin, my dad wanted no part of it. He just walked out on my pregnant mother and me.

My mom packed our bags and took us to New Jersey to live with my grandmother. My mom says I missed my dad and was old enough to recognize that he wasn't there anymore. I was sad, but she kept me busy. We would go to the boardwalk in Ocean City, and she signed me up for dance classes at the same place she went when she was a kid. I guess she thought it would be cute if I followed in her footsteps. Even then, though, I think I knew I wasn't the ballerina type.

If my mom wasn't sure, she definitely got the message at my first recital. My classmates and I practiced for weeks for the big performance, but when it was finally showtime I walked out with the group and plopped my ass down on the front of the stage. I refused to dance.

"Get up! Get up!" my mom instructed.

No response.

"Come on, honey . . ."

Nothing.

Then she got angry. "If you don't get up right now . . ."

Her threats had no effect on me. I didn't want to perform in front of all those people, and there was nothing anyone could do to convince me. The only show they got from me was when my mom finally gave up and I stuck my finger up my nose. I was up there pretty good, so I'm sure the crowd appreciated it. My mom didn't, however, and that was the end of dance class for me.

Shortly after my less than stellar performance, my dad decided he wanted us back. Colin was an infant, and taking care of two kids was an even larger task than just dealing with me, so my mom decided to give the relationship another shot. Plus, she still loved him. So we said good-bye to Grandma and moved back west to Clairemont.

To me, the time in Jersey felt like a vacation, but I'm sure for my mom it was anything but. Then, when we got back to California, life became even less fun for her. She and my dad bought a town house and had plans to buy a house shortly after, and for a while my dad made an effort to make this family work. But then, according to my mom, he started acting strange. He would stay out late partying and sometimes not come home at all. A year after we moved back to Clairmont, he was ready to take off again.

This time when he left, although I was young, I remember being put right in the middle of the split. Looking back, it was pretty intense stuff for a child. My dad asked me to go with him and my mom wanted me to stay with her. I knew I wanted to be with my mom but, being a kid, I didn't want to hurt anyone's feelings. My heart just wouldn't let me be honest. I couldn't say, "Daddy, I like Mommy more than you." So instead, when it came time to make the big decision, I balanced on a crack in the sidewalk and said, "I'm going to step on this crack and close my eyes and if I fall toward Mom I will go with her and if I fall toward Dad I will go with him."

I left it up to the gods to tilt the Earth in a way that made me fall in one direction. It was no longer up to me. No one could be upset.

I fell toward my mom and my dad took off.

After he left my brother and I were crying, so my mom took us down to the bay and we went to 7-Eleven and got Martinelli's apple juice (my favorite). We were walking down by the bay, sipping Martinelli's and still feeling sad, when a ladybug landed on my hand. I looked down and saw a thousand of them running around on the ground. I got really excited and sat down and started counting them as high as I could count, and before I knew it I started feeling better. From that day forward, ladybugs would be a symbol of happiness for me because on what was a terrible day, they provided a small amount of joy.

Throughout my childhood, my dad would pop in and out. My mom says I used to get upset about his absence and say, "Where's daddy?" and "How come daddy doesn't want to see me?"

My mom was *always* there for us. She worked at a doctor's office doing the payroll and organizational work, and with two kids, a husband who made her life more difficult, and a job that kept her busy all day, she was pretty stressed out. She always found time for us, though, and she always wanted the best for us kids. She knew we needed happy memories, and she did her best to provide them for us. A little help arrived in the form of my grandmother, who moved in right next door when I was about six years old. My grandfather moved to town, too, even though he and my grandmother were separated, and helped raise us. My mom made sure we had a family.

My dad, on the other hand, never excelled at parenting. During one Super Bowl Sunday, when I was about seven years old, Colin and I went to his house for the day. Sometimes my mom would go with us when we spent a day with him because he wasn't great at taking care of us.

This time, though, he was on his own and he failed miserably.

He didn't want to ruin his fun or have his children wreck his opportunity to watch the big game, so instead of letting us play inside he set us to play in the backyard while he had a big party in the house.

I snuck inside and called my mom and said, "Daddy is leaving us in the backyard. We're not allowed in the house."

She was pissed. My mom came and got us, and that was that. Over the next few years she would put up with his antics, but he was never going to be the father she wanted him to be. Truthfully, I wasn't sure he wanted us, or any sort of family at all. Every now and then he would get a second or third or fourth chance, but then one day he just gave up and disappeared for good.

⁓

*E*ven with my dad coming and going, I had a pretty normal childhood. My mom kept signing me up for activities (though she never tried to get me to take ballet classes again) and helping me find interests. But while she wanted me to get involved in the activities, she was good about letting me explore a little and find what I was really interested in doing with my free time.

At one point when I was still really young she started putting me in beauty pageants. All the little girls' faces were caked with makeup, but that wasn't me and my mom wasn't going to make me look like a Barbie if I didn't want to. I made it to the finals makeup-free but lost. Even at an early age, it was obvious that I was more the sporty type.

Later I took gymnastics, but I never figured out how to do a flip. I was afraid of heights and always felt like my leotard was riding up my crotch, so I knew that wasn't for me.

Then I tried Girl Scouts. Camping was awesome—I loved spending a weekend in the woods, telling ghost stories and eating junk food—but Girl Scouts wasn't really for me, either. I couldn't be around too many girls for long without getting annoyed. Also, the shoes we had to wear hurt my feet, and most of the activities were a pain in the ass. The worst part came when it was time to sell Girl Scout Cookies. I scarfed down all of them—the Thin Mints were the first to go—and forced my mom to pay for all the boxes. She didn't like that, so that was the end of my career as a Girl Scout.

In elementary school I finally started to find my niche. During recess all the girls would jump rope, and I was fascinated by it. This one girl, Jackie, was the best in the whole school. She was lightning fast and a pro at double Dutch. Someone would have a stopwatch and time her jumps per minute. She was out-of-control good, and I was impressed. I practiced my skills and worked to become Jackie-like on the playground. I never beat her, but one time I came really close, and that was good enough for me; it was such a great feeling just to be in her league.

But there's just so much time you can spend jumping rope before you start to lose your mind. I needed more excitement.

One day I was over at my best friend's house and she had to leave to go play in her soccer game at a field down the street from where I lived. I went, too, just to watch, but her team was short one person so they asked me to play. My friend, who maybe wasn't all that nice, was quick to point out that it was an organized league and you had to pay to be on the team.

I wanted to play so bad. I ran home and begged my mom to get me on that team. She agreed, and I immediately poured my heart and soul into soccer. Once I stepped on the field, I knew that this was the sport for me. With gymnastics, jumping rope, and dance something was missing. Turns out I just needed to play with balls. Who knew?

I loved soccer, and I was really good at it. I was in shorts, not a leotard, and I was kicking ass out there. I got really into kickball, too. All the kids at school played both sports, and I was the best of the girls and able to keep up with the boys. We played both soccer and kickball as often as possible after school and during PE and recess.

I also started playing softball. I loved getting down and dirty and coming home with scraped knees. I earned the nickname "Dodger" because I was so fast that I would dodge all the tags as I rounded the bases and come in safe every time. I wrote "Dodger" on the side of my helmet and played whenever I could.

Every month my elementary school held an assembly during which the teachers would give out awards. I always won for best athlete. It was great to be given a plaque in front of the whole school. My mom would beg me to wear a dress for the assembly, so I would leave the house all dressed up and then change into jeans when I got to school. Then, of course, my mom would show up at the assembly, see me not wearing the pretty dress I was wearing when I left the house, and get pissed off. But when the teacher handed me the award she'd forget all about my clothes.

My mom let me explore my options in life beginning at a young age, and when I found something I was good at she was very proud. Sometimes, though, that freedom backfired. Maybe having a father who wasn't around and a mother who worked long hours to put food on the table forced me to miss a few important conversations as a child. Maybe so much freedom to explore was too much for any child to handle. Either way, my exploratory side did get me in trouble every now and then.

Once, when I was around seven years old, I was playing with another little girl in my bedroom after school. A babysitter, who was probably in high school, was watching us. We were curious kids, so we often turned to this babysitter when we had a question about anything in life. Well, that day we decided to ask her about sex.

She had no problem opening up.

"First the mother and father take off all of their clothes . . ."

Our eyes lit up.

"Then the mommy and the daddy . . ."

Well, I probably don't need to tell you how it's done.

I always felt like I was more mature and advanced than other kids my age, but the kinds of details the babysitter provided were still pretty shocking for a seven-year-old.

My friend and I couldn't wait to put our new knowledge to the test. The next day she came over and we went upstairs and did as we'd been told.

We built a little house inside my closet and stripped down like Mommy and Daddy would. I was the mom and she was the dad (I wasn't really sure how a dad was supposed to act, so being the mom seemed more up my alley). Turned out, it didn't really matter which role I was playing, because when my mom walked in and found two naked little girls humping in the closet she freaked out and started screaming at us. It was really embarrassing.

My mom started blaming everyone in the world for us ending up in the buff. She blamed my friend. She blamed herself. She blamed the babysitter. She didn't really blame me, though. I was a good girl in her eyes, so it definitely wasn't my fault. (Her words, not mine.) The truth is, I didn't know what sex was and I didn't know any better, but I did know I had a rebellious streak somewhere inside me. I just hadn't unleashed it quite yet. That afternoon of nude humping wasn't my fault, but it was certainly the start of something that my mom knew she had to put a stop to.

That evening we had a humiliating sit-down meeting with all the parents. My friend got sent away to an all-girls school, and I was stuck playing house all by myself.

CHAPTER 3

A Friend in Need

$\mathcal{E}$ven though I was good at sports and had an amazing ability to get girls to take their clothes off, I struggled at a young age to find a group where I really fit in.

Don't get me wrong—people liked me. I'd have a roller-skating party for my birthday and everyone would show up to watch me do the limbo. I was competitive and always had to be the best, uh, limbo-er, but still, the other girls thought I was cool. In fact, I had two friends in elementary school who would actually fight over who got to be my best friend. I told one that she could be my Monday-Tuesday-Wednesday friend and the other that she could be a Thursday-Friday-Saturday friend. Problem solved. That solution was short-lived, though, because girls are crazy at that age. Well, girls are crazy at any age, but young, insecure girls are especially crazy. Ultimately, elementary school girls hate other girls and it's only a matter of time before you go from having two girls fight over you to them deciding that instead of sharing time with you, they can just become each other's every-day friend.

At the end of the day, I was always searching for friends and looking for my place in this world.

Growing up, I got bullied a little bit by some of the boys. Maybe they just liked me but, flirty or not, I was not going to take it. I was tough and didn't let anyone push me around. One time a kid was messing with me, calling me "horsehair" and "freckle face" and getting all the kids to laugh at me. Finally, I couldn't take it anymore. I picked up a handful of sand and threw it right in the boy's eyes. He chased me around, yelling and screaming, but I outran him and he learned his lesson.

The girls weren't much friendlier. One girl in my neighborhood who was at least three or four years older than I was (that's a lot when you're in elementary school) picked on me all the time. One day she took a bamboo stick and just kept hitting me with it over and over. I didn't want her to have the satisfaction of knowing she was hurting me so I kept saying it didn't hurt. She kept hitting and I just stood there and stared back at her. Once she gave up and went home, I ran to my room and cried my eyes out. Another time she stomped on my toe so hard it bled, but I stood my ground.

That's just how I was. I never backed down. Even though people judged me and called me names, I was always open to being friends with anyone. It was always the popular kids who were giving me a hard time, so when it came to finding real friends I tended to drift toward the kids who were less accepted—the nerds, the kids in wheelchairs, and the loners of the school. I felt more comfortable with them. I was never ashamed to be seen with a certain kind of person; if they were nice, I wanted to be their friend.

I grew up in a diverse neighborhood, so I didn't see race or ethnicity at all. My mom taught me that everyone is equal and beautiful in his or her own way. But there are walls and divisions in our society, and sometimes discovering them is hard for a kid.

When I was eight years old my mom took me to Target to buy a birthday present for my friend Lisa, a black girl who was one of my good friends from the neighborhood. We walked down the aisle with all the Barbie dolls, and there was Malibu Barbie, and all sorts of blonde dolls that looked a lot like me—but not so much like Lisa. I knew the company made a black Barbie, but that particular store didn't have it. I didn't even know if Lisa cared about that sort of thing, but I started to cry because there were no black Barbies. It was so sad to see that something as great as Barbie was only available in white, when I wanted to buy a black Barbie for my friend. Now, of course, the Barbie people have a wide variety of dolls that are available at almost any store. Walk into your local Target and there's probably a Tramp Stamp Barbie and an Obama Barbie and an Octo-Barbie with eight kids running around. But at the time, it was very disturbing to only see one face on the shelf.

As I got a little older the racial divisions at my elementary school became so obvious that I was actually ashamed to be white. I hated the white kids, so I started telling people I was black. Whether they believed me—with my blonde hair and blue eyes—or not didn't really matter. I just didn't want to associate with the white kids.

Another good friend of mine at the time was a Mexican boy named Chris. I think I was probably his only friend. He sort of just blended in and went unnoticed by most of the other kids, but I thought he was the greatest. He would come over and call my mom Ms. Wilkinson with his little accent and I thought it was so cute.

I took him skating for the first time and loved getting him to do all sorts of fun things that he'd never done before. He was very religious and sheltered, so I felt I needed to open his eyes to other important things in the world—like Ouija boards.

The whole concept of Ouija boards scared the shit out of him because of his religious background; he wanted to stay away from this devil game. But I convinced him to give it a shot, of course. We went to my room, sat down, and turned the lights out. With the Ouija board balanced on our laps, we asked it our important questions.

"Will Kendra have big boobs?"

The dial slowly inched its way to spell out Y-E-S. (Damn right!)

"Will Target ever sell black Barbies?"

Y-E-S. (Good to know.)

Then it was Chris's turn. I didn't really believe in the powers of the Ouija, but sometimes it seemed like odd things happened when we started playing with it.

"Will Chris die?"

It seemed like a perfectly good question for a little kid to ask.

We were very quiet and the atmosphere in the room felt a little scary as the dial slowly moved to the Y. When it spelled out Y-E-S, Chris freaked out and ran home.

A few months later we were playing kickball at school with a bunch of kids when Chris started acting really weird. We played kickball almost every day at recess, so he knew the rules as well as any other kid. But when it was his turn, he kicked the ball and ran across the field to second base instead of to first. He was on my team and a good friend, so instead of laughing at him like the other kids I corrected him and pointed him in the direction of first base for next time.

Then when he was up again he kicked the ball and ran straight to third base. More laughter from the other kids.

I didn't get it. Why wasn't he running to first? What was his problem?

The next day he didn't come to school. Then a week went by and there was no sign of Chris. We started asking the teacher about him, and eventually she told us all that Chris had a brain tumor and would not be back.

Chris was in the hospital for a while and then he went to a special school where I got to visit him one time. He was in a wheelchair and didn't look healthy at all, and I was so sad for him. His illness seemed to be happening so fast. One day we were playing with the Ouija board in my room and the next he was in the hospital.

Shortly after I visited him, he died. Even though I knew he was sick, I didn't realize he was going to die, so I felt like I didn't get to say good-bye. It was heartbreaking to lose him.

Maybe that day with the Ouija board he knew he was sick, and asking if he was going to die was his way of trying to tell me. Or maybe we were just two kids having fun and it was an odd coincidence. Either way, the prediction came true. I've never touched a Ouija board since, because it reminds me of Chris and brings back all sorts of sad feelings.

Chris will always have a special place in my heart. I think about him all the time, and if you asked a Ouija board if I'll always remember him, I can tell you for certain that the answer would be Y-E-S.

———

Outside of my few friends at school, I also turned to odd people around my neighborhood for companionship.

Next door to the development where we lived was a retirement community that as kids we kindly referred to as the "old-people complex." The other kids in the neighborhood and I loved it there, and we bugged the elderly people all the time.

One of my friends and I really bonded with an older Asian man named Yen who lived there. After school we would go and knock on Yen's door together, or sometimes I went by myself. I never told my mom about the visits, though, because I knew she wouldn't approve. And if she was going to say no, then why ask, right?

Yen didn't speak a word of English and I didn't speak Yen, yet somehow we communicated. He would always ask me to come in, but I knew better than that. Instead he would come outside and watch me as I performed all the cool things I was able to do at the time: I'd jump rope, bounce a ball off my knee, and do a few cartwheels, and the two of us would just look at each other and talk with our eyes. It seemed pretty normal. I felt closer to this old man than I did to most of the kids in my school.

This was also the case with an older woman in the neighbor-hood. She and I were supertight. I would go to her house and get something cold to drink and play with all her birds and cats. I would help her carry groceries, too, which made me feel like I was doing a good deed.

It's funny that I was so into helping my elderly neighbor, because if my mom asked me to carry groceries I would get mad and try anything to get out of it. Doing it for this woman, though, was no problem. I liked helping others when no one was looking or expected anything from me, but to do the same for my mom, who expected me to help around the house, always seemed like a pain in the ass. I would want to do stuff to make her happy and surprise her with good deeds, but the second she asked me to help her I wasn't interested.

When my grandmother, Mary, moved from New Jersey to live next door, she and I had a similar relationship. She was very loving, but she wasn't the kind of pushover grandparent who spoils kids. She was more like a second mother to me.

My grandfather, her ex-husband, also took over some of the fatherly duties. He would take me to soccer games and occa-sionally pick me up from school. In the car he would sing "You Are My Sunshine" and I would tell him to shut up because I thought it was embarrassing.

He was a World War II veteran, so he would take us to air shows to watch the Blue Angels, and to the naval base in San Diego. We spent a lot of time there and attended all the special events they held at the base—Easter egg hunts, Mother's Day brunch, and the annual barbecue where they served amazing Mexican food. Of course the Fourth of July was like his Christmas. He would say the Pledge of Allegiance every day, but on the Fourth of July he would raise a flag in the yard and, with his hand over his heart, sing the national anthem loud enough for the entire neighborhood to hear. All the kids would laugh at him, myself included, but he didn't care. He loved his country and made sure we grew up appreciating the military.

My grandfather taught my brother and me to say "please" and "thank you" to others and to not put our elbows on the table, and I think he was the first person on the planet to recycle. I would accompany him on the drive to the recycling center with a million cans in tow, and more often than not he would pull over along the way to scoop up more recyclables from the side of the road. He'd swerve across six lanes of traffic and drive in reverse a hundred yards if he spotted a can on the road. It was crazy, but he was set on teaching me to treat others with respect and to care about the world.

However, all my values and manners went out the window when it came to my brother, Colin. When we were little we did *not* get along. We are three years apart, so in elementary school he was always following me around and copying my every move. I hated him for being a little tagalong so I was constantly yelling at him and beating him up. I was always so nice to everyone else and made a point of protecting the weaker kids in school, but my brother was my personal punching bag.

Aside from a few fights with my brother, though, I was a good kid, and a pretty normal one at that. I was always outside, building forts and tree houses, digging for dinosaur bones, and using my imagination to make my own fun. Friends or no friends, old Asian dudes or little Mexican boys, dad or no dad,

I was going to enjoy life and do whatever I had to do to be a happy kid.

Everything was going smoothly until I graduated elementary school and moved on to middle school. It was then that I could have used a father, or at the very least a friend who was a good influence. Because when I turned thirteen, I was no longer my grandfather's little sunshine.

CHAPTER 4

A Perfect Misfit

*W*hen I got to middle school I thought I was very mature. Some of my best friends were senior citizens, so it only made sense that I would think I was too grown-up for the kids in my own grade. I was a tiny blonde girl running around in soccer shorts, but inside I was wise beyond my years.

I wanted to know more about everything I was beginning to be told to avoid. Sex, drugs, alcohol—it all had my teenage brain working a mile a minute. I was ready to explore the world, but my mom had other plans for me. She was strict, man.

The first real parties I ever went to were at Skateworld, where I had birthday parties as a kid. My mom loved it then, but once I got to middle school her opinion changed. She thought it was a place where bad kids hung out, and she was right. The middle school girls always dressed skanky to go to Skateworld, and before the end of the night they'd usually find someone to hook up with. Everyone my age stayed there until it closed and then hung out at a spot in the neighborhood until all hours. But I had a curfew, so at nine o'clock my mom rolled up to Skateworld in her red Jeep Grand Cherokee to drag me away from all the fun. I was embarrassed and, in my mind, it was totally unfair. I wanted to do what my friends were doing; instead, I sat at home wondering what I was missing. Then, in school on Monday, everyone would talk about who kissed who or who gave head to who, and I'd missed all of it!

I couldn't live with her rules. I was ready to be a rebel and make my own choices. She pulled me out of Skateworld one too many times and I decided I would not let her ruin my night again. So when the next big party came around, I didn't bother to tell her about it. Instead I just ran away. I left the house when she wasn't paying attention and spent the night getting drunk on Mickey's malt liquor in the Mervyn's parking lot with no intention of going home again. A few hours in I was pretty hammered, and a friend thought I would sober up with some coffee. No luck. That just made me more wired and gave me a stomachache. It was a disaster.

At the end of the night when the party was over I had nowhere to go but home. My big plan to run away didn't even last the night.

Even when I was in elementary school, I'd dreamed about running away. I would get a couple people in on my plan and we would talk about saving our money and getting on a bus to leave town. We weren't trying to run away from anything specific; we were more interested in running toward something. We wanted to be adults. We wanted adventure. It would take us weeks to save our pennies, and when we finally had our money together we would all chicken out at the last minute.

This time was sort of the same. I was going to run away to make my own decisions and be my own boss, but when all the other kids went home, I had no choice but to do the same.

My mom was very mad when I arrived home, of course. She yelled, grounded me, and threatened to never let me see certain friends again. I just stood there and listened and showed no emotion. I didn't care what she had to say. The bottom line was that I was back under her rules and already plotting my next escape.

One of the next parties I was invited to was down at the beach. Based on my recent behavior, my mom wasn't so sure I should go.

"Pleeeeeeeease," I begged, knowing full well that I was going to go no matter what she said.

"Are the girl's parents going to be there?"

"Of course." (Fingers crossed behind my back.)

"Okay, but I'm picking you up at ten P.M.," she said. "No funny business."

It was a camping party and everyone—boys and girls—had tents and was allowed to spend the night. Again, we were all drinking (it was the latest middle school fad), and for most kids it didn't matter because they could just sleep it off. I still had my curfew, so my fun had to end early.

When my mom came to pick me up she could tell that I had been drinking. She could smell it on my breath, and she was furious.

"That's it!" she screamed. "You are spending the night in juvenile hall."

My younger brother, who was probably ten years old at the time, was in the car and he was freaking out. I, on the other hand, was cool as a cucumber. Maybe the alcohol blurred my ability to fear my mom's threats, but I wasn't scared of her. We pulled up to our local juvie and she yanked me out of the car and dragged me inside.

"Officer!" my mom yelled. "I just picked up my daughter and she's been drinking. She's twelve years old and I want you to keep her."

The two cops behind the desk looked at each other in amazement. The expressions on their faces said it all: *Who is this crazy lady and what are we supposed to do with this kid?*

Colin saw their guns and was even more freaked out. But there was nothing they could do. The place was full of real criminals. They were never going to keep me there. The officers took me in the back and tried to scare me by threatening me, and then they let me go.

"What are you doing?" my mom said. "Aren't you going to keep her?"

Uh, no, Mom.

She drove me home and that was the end of it. She was losing control of me and she knew it.

It was a slow but steady process. A missed curfew here, a night of drinking there. Day by day, as I made my way through the seventh grade, I was turning into the kind of kid who would become totally uncontrollable, and I could see my mother unraveling.

Things took another turn for the worse when I expanded my social network outside of school and found an older crowd of people who wanted to hang out with me. My walk home from school wasn't long, but on the way there were a few areas where kids and even young adults gathered after school or work to chill.

One day an older guy, probably around twenty years old, was standing outside his apartment complex with a few other people, all in their late teens. I was friendly, so I stopped and said hello and we started talking. Eventually he invited me upstairs to his apartment to hang out with his friends.

It was a small apartment, with a living room and a kitchen on the left and a hallway with two bedrooms on the right. There were half a dozen guys and girls sitting on the couch, talking and drinking. It seemed like a fine place and I was excited that this older group had welcomed me. I clicked with them immediately, and I felt cool hanging out with older kids, so I really felt like I belonged with this crowd. I knew I'd found my place and quickly became a regular.

One of the girls in the apartment was a hot girl who had recently moved into my neighborhood. I remember seeing her around and thinking she was so beautiful. I wanted to be her friend but, more important, I wanted to be just like her. Listening to her that day in the apartment, to my virgin ears at least, she sounded very experienced when it came to sex.

A short while later she and I went to the beach together and she told me about all the sex she had had and how it felt and how to do it. The way she described it was way more detailed than anything my babysitter had ever mentioned.

All the guys at the house would laugh at me because I was still a virgin, and everything she was saying sounded so amazing. When she was done talking, only one thought went through my thirteen-year-old head: *I need to have sex right now.*

I ran home from the beach as fast as I could and immediately called Samuel, a friend of mine who was in my class at school. He was a tall, skinny white boy. I had a little crush on him, but he was always more of a friend than a boyfriend. My family loved him because he was a good kid—the perfect kind of kid to be allowed in my room without my mom questioning what was going on up there.

"Hey, Samuel, what are you up to?" I asked.

"Nothing."

"You want to come over?"

"Sure, why not."

"And have sex."

I think he must have run out of his room before he even hung up the phone because his mom dropped him off at my house in what seemed like a split second. He slipped past my mom and grandma, who were downstairs in the kitchen, and came right up to my room.

I shut the door behind him and we hopped onto the top bunk and started kissing. He was shaking a little, and I could tell he was nervous. We were both virgins, but I wanted so bad to not be a virgin that my fear went completely out the window.

Lying on his back, Samuel took a condom out of his pocket and slipped his pants off. I don't know where he got that condom, but I wouldn't be surprised if it had spent a year or two in his pocket.

I climbed on top of him, but we had no idea what we were doing. I just knew that once I started bleeding I was no longer a virgin, so I watched and waited and, after a minute or so, there was blood.

We stopped—two unsatisfied, sexually frustrated teenagers. But I wasn't a virgin anymore and I was very happy about that. It was literally the best time of my life, at that moment. I was a fucking woman!

Samuel's mom dropped him off a boy and picked him up a few hours later a man. Things were weird between us afterward and we never had sex again, but none of that mattered to me. I couldn't wait to go back to that apartment and tell everyone.

———

Losing my virginity was just the beginning of me living on the edge. That apartment turned out to be a window to a very bad world for me. My first day there, they handed me a beer. It was only my second or third time drinking (after my mom caught me that one time she always smelled my breath after I'd been out). They weren't trying to pressure me into anything; they just assumed I would want one, and they were right. I cracked open that beer and pretended I drank all the time.

As time went on I started spending more and more of my afternoons at the apartment. I felt comfortable with these older, more experienced people—way more comfortable than I did with the kids at my school, where I sort of floated around between crowds, never really finding a group or clique to call my own. These guys, while significantly older, welcomed me with open arms. I was like the little sister who would do anything that they never had.

And when I say that I would do anything, I mean *anything*.

They did all sorts of drugs at the apartment—pot, coke, LSD, and various kinds of pills. Everyone there was getting fucked up all the time.

I knew a little about drugs before meeting these people. We learned about drugs in the D.A.R.E. program in school, and it was common knowledge that drugs were bad. My mom didn't really think I would get into drugs because I was so into sports, so she pretty much stayed away from the topic, but even with the little information I had at that age I knew in the back of my mind that it was wrong and dangerous. Somehow, though, it still sounded more fun that bad.

So when I fell in love with this apartment-complex crowd, I began experimenting. Sure, in sixth grade I'd once tried to smoke nutmeg (which didn't work), but this time it was for real.

The first time they broke out coke at the apartment, just looking at it made my eyes bulge out of my head with excitement. I knew it was bad, but I liked bad. I wanted to try anything and everything, regardless of what it would do to me. I thought it was cool, and I couldn't wait to give it a shot.

Someone poured the coke on a tray on the table, and it looked like snow falling from the sky. One guy cut it up into lines and then everyone took turns snorting it. I watched and took notes in my head on how to do it—I didn't want to look stupid.

One by one they went around and sniffed it right up, and then it was my turn.

"Do you want to try some?" one guy asked as he passed me the rolled-up dollar bill they were using.

"Okay."

I couldn't have been more ready, but I guess my face was saying something my brain wasn't because they all started laughing. I knew I was young and the tone of my "okay" probably tipped them off that it was my first time, but my head told me I was ready. I didn't have a voice in my head telling me no. I didn't picture my mother's disappointment. I just saw an opportunity to try something new.

So, despite their laughter, or maybe out of spite, I shoved the bill up my nose, bent over, and snorted my first line of cocaine.

I chased the coke with a beer and my throat started feeling funny. I was told, amid more laughter, that this was a "drip," and that it happens with coke. It felt like a big ball of shit going down my throat. I couldn't swallow, and for a few seconds it was absolutely terrible. Once that went away, though, I started feeling really good. I did a little more that day, and after that I wanted to keep doing it over and over again. I felt like I could stop at any time, but I just wanted more.

As one might expect, my trouble outside of school led to trouble inside school as well. It was inevitable that my afternoon activities at the apartment would cause me to make bad decisions throughout the rest of the day, too.

I was on drugs, doing coke all the time. I started to act like the bad girl in school, skipping class and smoking cigarettes, and once I got that reputation I felt like I had to live up to it.

I snapped and became someone I wasn't—a real problem child.

I would do all sorts of crazy things to fit my new persona, like take markers and color all over myself or show up at school in a bikini.

"You can't leave the house like that," my mom would say.

"It's bikini day at school," I would reply as I left the house, before she could realize that no school would have a bikini day.

All the kids laughed when they saw me in the bikini. I loved it.

The school obviously had a dress code and, as it turns out, bikinis were not acceptable. I knew the rules. I didn't like the rules, so I made my own. This stunt earned me strike one.

Later I was assigned a "how-to" school project. We had to teach the class one of our skills, so I brought in a baseball bat to teach the class how to play softball, because even though I was doing drugs, sports were still my strength.

But my walking down the hallway with marker all over my body, my hair out of control, baseball bat in hand, freaked out some of the adults. Some of the other kids were scared, too. I was a total psycho and I loved when people were scared of me. As I walked to class, a teacher came up to me and nicely asked me about the bat. She could have yelled and dragged my ass to the principal's office, but she was sweet.

I was not.

I yelled and screamed that the bat was for a project, and nearly threw it at her. It took three teachers to settle me down.

Strike two.

At the time, my best friend was a girl named Brittany. She was that girl who everyone wanted to be friends with. She was in the cool, rebellious, Skateworld crowd, but was respected by the preppies and goody-goodies, too. She asked me to eat lunch with her one day and we just clicked. Her group had their hair scrunched with mousse and their bangs flipped out to their eyebrows, and very quickly I started to look and act like her. Now she's religious and into God, but back then *we* were the bad girls.

We'd hide in bushes and jump out and scare people when they walked by, and we did a lot of experimenting together. When we heard about bulimia, we wondered what it would be like to throw up our food, so we went to the bathroom together and puked. That was just one of the many stupid things we did.

Brittany and I also used to steal liquor from my grandmother's house, take it to the local pool in my neighborhood, and drink it. It was dangerous and fun but we usually took only a very small amount, so the impact was minimal.

One day toward the end of seventh grade, I felt like causing a little trouble and taking our petty theft to the next level. I wanted to bring alcohol to school.

I knew it was wrong, but I didn't think it was all that bad. It's not like I'd be hurting anyone, right? Plus, I thought I was cool, a step ahead of the other kids. I thought I knew something they didn't about life.

I waited until my grandmother was out running errands one afternoon, then grabbed the spare key from where my mom always left it, snuck inside my grandmother's house, and made my way to the liquor cabinet. The house was empty and quiet, but I acted like I was a professional robber, hiding behind couches and other furniture while making my way toward the cabinet.

Really, though, getting the alcohol was usually very simple. I just had to go in there, pop open the liquor cabinet, and take whatever looked liked it would be missed the least. But that day I thought it would be fun to make it more of an adventure, so I acted stealthily and snagged all the little plastic airplane bottles of alcohol I could fit in my hands.

The next morning I put the bottles in my backpack and was off to school. I drank some vodka in the bathroom and went to class drunk. People expected me to be off the wall, so none of the teachers suspected I was under the influence. Unfortunately, I gave a bottle to a kid who couldn't handle his liquor (what kind of seventh grader was he?) and the teachers caught him. He got called to the office, and of course he ratted me out.

I was so pissed. No matter how bad I was, I never ratted anyone out. If there was one rule in life that I actually did follow, it was *You don't rat someone out.*

A guidance counselor and a security guard came and pulled me out of class. When a security guard was there, you knew you were in trouble. When I got to the principal's office, there was a police officer waiting for me (even worse).

"Have you been drinking?" he asked.

"No, of course not."

"Where did you get the alcohol?"

"What alcohol?"

"Listen, we can give you a lie detector and ask you these questions if you'd like."

They probably weren't really going to do that, but it was enough to make me cave . . . almost.

"I got the alcohol out of the Dumpster in the alley," I said, coming clean about having the booze but still lying because I didn't want to involve my family.

They'd heard enough. Strike three.

Summer was around the corner, but for me it started a little early. They kicked me out of school and told me to never come back.

Those were the rules, whether I liked them or not.

CHAPTER 5

Summer Druggin'

*W*ith school out of the way I had the summer to live a little. Meanwhile, my mom was begging anyone who would listen to let me back into my regular school for eighth grade. She even went to a hearing and tried her hardest to get me reinstated.

I didn't care. While she was fighting for my right to an education, I was at the beach, playing soccer and fighting for my right to party. I also spent more and more time at that apartment and fell further in love with cocaine.

I didn't have a source of money at the time and I never wanted to ask my mom for cash. Even though I was always up to no good, deep down I had a good heart. I knew my mom was struggling to make ends meet, so I wouldn't even take lunch money if I could get along without it by eating my friends' food or bumming money from them. I always wanted to be a person who earned money, instead of just taking it from my mom.

In the beginning of my drug phase I would go to the apartment near my school looking cute and smile big until one of the guys gave me coke or weed for free. But as I got more and more into drugs, the smile just wasn't cutting it. I needed to come up with money to support my habit. I began to occasionally ask my mother for lunch money or for some cash to see a movie, and then I'd use it to buy drugs. Other times I would sneak into my grandmother's house and steal from her purse. I didn't think she would catch on, and she never said anything, so I figured I was in the clear.

With my new income and no school to pretend to worry about, I was free to enjoy summer to the fullest, and I started to really lose control. I think I would have gone off the deep end completely if not for my love of sports. That was the one thing that kept me sane. Even when drugs were taking over and causing me to make bad decisions, in my heart I still enjoyed playing sports.

That summer I was in a youth soccer league, and when I was on the field I was a different person. I was focused. I was an athlete. I wasn't the girl who got kicked out of school. I was like Jekyll and Hyde; on the field I was a good girl, but when I was at that apartment, I did lots of coke. I never even mentioned soccer to the people I hung out with in the apartment. They weren't into it, and I didn't want to talk about it. I wanted to keep those worlds separate.

But as summer dragged on and my coke habit turned into an obsession, soccer started to take a backseat. Instead of resting up the night before a big game I would be out partying. Sometimes I'd even go right from the apartment to the game, high on cocaine. On those occasions I'd run around the field like a crazy girl, heart racing, drenched in sweat, and out of control until I started to come down. Then I'd lose all my energy and running would become hard. I was also smoking cigarettes pretty often (I stole those from my grandmother, too), so when I wasn't tearing around like mad, I was coughing up phlegm and wheezing my way down the field.

Despite the toll the drugs took, for the most part I was still a pretty good player. There was a traveling team that I really wanted to be on. It was expensive, and I knew my mom couldn't afford it, but I tried out anyway and made the team. When my mom told me I couldn't go, it was heartbreaking. When I realized I was stuck playing on the local team, my interest level dropped even further.

It was around this time that I got into acid, which was a big drug to do at the time because you could get it for five dollars a pop. It was going around the neighborhood, and one of the guys at the apartment complex hooked me up with some.

"It's amazing," the guy who sold it to me said. "You'll see trolls in trees and rainbows and smiley faces everywhere."

Sounds cool.

I took the acid and went to Skateworld. Like many roller-skating rinks, Skateworld has a lot of lights flashing all over the place, so I had a really bad trip. There were no rainbows; it just felt like the lights were attacking me and the walls were closing in on me. People were messing with me and telling me I had spiders all over my body. I bugged out.

My mom came to get me, but luckily I held it together and she didn't notice that anything was wrong. She took me home and I ran up to my room, where I sat on my bed and stayed awake all night.

It was only a matter of time before I took my newest habit to the soccer field. I dropped acid before a game one time and it was *not* fun. (Okay, it was a little fun.) My mom drove me to the game, and during the car ride the acid kicked in. Things that usually didn't move were moving, and things that should have been moving fast, like other cars, seemed to be moving really slowly.

Once the game started things got even worse. At one point the ball went out of bounds and I was supposed to throw it in. To this day I'm not sure if I ever actually threw the ball onto the field. I just remember picking it up and staring at it, amazed at all its beautiful black and white dots.

My mom was at the game, but she didn't yell at me or punish me. It's hard to say if she just didn't realize I was on drugs or if she pretended she didn't know to make herself feel better. Either way, she kept quiet. I think she knew I was in trouble but she was getting tired of yelling at me and trying to control me. There was nothing she could do, so she sat back and prayed I would learn to make better decisions in the future while denying how bad the problem was at the moment. I guess she handled things a little backwards: her anger came first, and then the denial phase started.

I felt a little bad. I hated not playing well, and I obviously wasn't at my best on acid. But the guilt wore off pretty quickly. I just made sure I got my hands on some coke, weed, or alcohol, and every bad thought immediately left my mind.

Along with regular sports, I went through an extreme-sports phase that summer. I got really into skateboarding and thought I was pretty awesome because after a couple months of practice

I could drop in on a half-pipe. But learning how to skateboard and do tricks only occasionally kept me from doing drugs.

Right near the park where I went to skate was another park—the park we did drugs in. I'd walk with my skateboard through the drug park to get to the skateboarding area, and plenty of times I never made it there. I'd stop and get high, and my day would be shot. I'd have the skateboard in my hand and I would choose to do drugs instead.

The skateboard park was also next to Horizon Christian Fellowship Church, and the preachers would come out every so often and try to talk to the other skaters and me about God. I think they thought the skating park was where the bad kids hung out—little did they know.

My family wasn't very religious, but I was always interested in what the preachers had to say; one time they even convinced me to come in and listen to a sermon. There was a small part of me that wanted to follow in their path and be a good kid, because deep down I *was* a good kid, but at that point in my life, nothing was going to save me.

I was pretty much fucked up every day that summer, and then when school started, I wasn't exactly motivated to turn things around. Even though my mom begged and pleaded to get me back into my regular school, I was forced to go to a "special" school for problem kids. There were kids who brought guns to school, gangbangers, and me, an innocent-looking little girl with an attitude problem and a growing love for drugs.

It wasn't even a school. It was just a big room in a shopping center where the other outcasts and I sat every day. We were all just dumped there, like garbage. I hated it. I wasn't learning anything (not that I wanted to). I knew I deserved to be there, and I guess I belonged with that crowd—actually, a part of me thought it was cool to be at the bad school—but I felt caged in.

I wasn't comfortable there. I needed to be out in the world, exploring what life had to offer. I couldn't be locked up with delinquents all day. Yeah, maybe I got into a little trouble, but I knew how to handle myself.

I felt it was time for me to be out on my own. I was a free spirit who couldn't be held back. So I stopped going to school just before spring break and ran away from home. I ran all the way around the corner to my friend Brittany's house. My mom was worried, and she reported me missing. She called all around town looking for me. She even called Brittany's house, but her mom, who answered the phone, didn't know I was there. I would sneak in and out of her house, doing drugs at all hours with the guys at the apartment, coming and going as I pleased.

My time as a runaway lasted about a month. Then my mom, with my grandmother's help, wised up. One evening they called Brittany's mother, and her mom insisted I wasn't there. At two A.M. they called again and asked her to just check Brittany's room and make sure.

Busted. My mom and grandma came and picked me up and took me home, kicking and screaming.

I don't know how my mom did it, but somehow she talked to the right people and convinced them to let me pass the eighth grade. I finished up at the strip-mall school and enrolled in some summer school classes, and with barely a 2.0 grade point average I was officially admitted as a freshman at Clairemont High School in the fall of 1999.

CHAPTER 6

Not-so-Fresh Feeling

Freshman year was sort of a fresh start: New school. New kids. New teachers. Most kids would have looked at it as an opportunity to turn things around, and I guess I started out seeing it that way. I was involved with activities—I joined the junior varsity soccer team, and I was obsessed with putting together the homecoming float—but it was hard for me to take school seriously, especially since right from the beginning the teachers weren't taking *me* seriously.

I had a perverted math teacher who made inappropriate comments to me all the time. He told me that if I wore a short skirt to open house and told all the parents about the stuff we were learning in class, he would give me an A for the semester. It was like I was asked to be a fourteen-year-old spokesmodel for math class. I didn't even know what we were learning, so he had to write it down for me. But I showed up to parents' night, looked cute, and watched that old man get wood while I talked about isosceles triangles. I got the A.

Then there was another teacher, who took my dyed red hair and tiny cutoff shorts as a sign that I was stupid. My grades weren't so great—I was pretty much hanging on by a thread except for math class—but the guy didn't even want to give me a chance, and I hated him for it. Not only was he a jerk, but he was also a narc: he would run a tape recorder during class because he wanted proof to take to the principal when the kids were acting out of line.

One day he had us go around the room and say what we wanted to be when we were older. When it was my turn, I said that I wanted to be a marine biologist. I loved the ocean and going to the aquarium, and I had a thing for sharks and whales. So at the time, marine biologist seemed like a decent plan.

He laughed in my face, and the whole class laughed with him.

"Do you really think you can be a marine biologist?" he asked in front of the whole class.

I wasn't embarrassed. I was mad. I got up and threw my chair to the ground. "Fuck you, motherfucker!" I screamed before storming out of class.

I didn't care who pissed me off—I never backed down. And I sure as hell wasn't going to sit there and take this from him.

When my mom heard what happened she was on my side. She charged into the school yelling and screaming, livid that a teacher would crush a little girl's dreams like that when he should've been motivating kids like me and pointing us in the right direction.

I think he eventually apologized, but the damage was done. Between the math teacher giving me good grades for being cute and the other teacher never even giving me a chance to succeed, I quickly lost interest in school again. No one there was supporting me. Sure, my mom would fight for me, but I needed more than that. I needed to feel like I could do something with my life. I needed a reason to be in school, and I just couldn't find one.

Around then I was introduced to a second bad group of kids. I met them through school. A few of them went to Claire-mont, but some of them were older. They all hung out at "the square"—an outdoor mall/movie theater near the high school— and they were all trouble.

My old group from the apartment was into drugs and just chilling, and I still hung out with them from time to time. But this new group was into doing drugs and tagging their names on walls, breaking shit, and fighting. They were a rough crew. I liked being tough—no one is going to tell a girl anything she doesn't want to hear if she's in the tough crowd.

My new group wasn't really a gang, but it was pretty close. On a typical night out with them, I'd ask my mom to drop me off at the movies, and instead of actually seeing a movie I would go around back and watch them spray-paint their tags on the wall behind the theater. I never did the tagging. I couldn't— literally; I was terrible with the spray can. But I liked being part of the group and I thought the graffiti was cool. I also liked that with these people behind me, nobody could fuck with me.

This group did drugs, too, and along with coke they did crystal meth. Crystal was harder, dirtier, and more powerful. I went to a party with them one night and they were all smoking it. They offered me some, so I took it (I wasn't really one to say no to anything). I inhaled the crystal meth and within seconds my heart was pounding. I felt unstoppable—like I could knock down a wall with my bare hands. I was like the Incredible Hulk trapped inside a five-foot-four, 115-pound girl. It felt good, but I also felt a little gross when I came down, sweaty and dirty, and saw the sunrise. I was talking fast, I got paranoid, and in general I felt like a crackhead. When I ran out of people to talk to I found a piece of paper and wrote down all my thoughts.

After running into my friend Sarah that night, I ended up sleeping at her house. She was in the crew with Brittany, and she only sometimes hung out with the tagger guys, but I needed a place to crash so Sarah invited me over. I was wired, though, so while she was sleeping I wrote her an eight-page letter about our friendship. It was nuts. I literally couldn't catch my breath all night. When the sun came up and I was still awake, I felt awful, just completely out of control.

But even with all the bad feelings that came from doing crystal that night, as soon as I was back in a position to do it again, I did. I didn't get addicted, though. I did a lot of crystal, but in my head I knew I could stop whenever I wanted to. I just didn't see a reason for stopping yet.

I started dating a guy in the group named Tony. He was a tall, dark, skinny half-Mexican guy with short brown hair. He wore baggy clothes, smoked cigarettes, and was one of the leaders of the tagger group. No one messed with him—he would knock someone out just for looking at him funny. He was tough and powerful, and I thought that was pretty hot. He was nineteen and I was fourteen and I thought we made a good couple.

One night I met Tony in a park where we sometimes went to drink and smoke weed, and we had sex on a park bench.

It was the first time I'd had sex since I lost my virginity with my buddy from seventh grade. Only a year and a half had passed, but I was a world away from where I was back then. I was now doing any drug I could get my hands on and having sex out in the open, and none of it seemed unnatural.

From that night on, I went everywhere with Tony. We did lots of drugs and had lots of sex. I wasn't quite sure if I enjoyed the sex. Most of the time I would have sex just to have it; it was more of an ego boost than anything.

I changed my look drastically that year. I shaved my eyebrows and drew them in, gelled my hair down, and overall looked pretty scary. I'd walk around the hallways at school thinking I was so cool, knowing my new group had my back so I could do whatever I wanted.

This sense of freedom allowed me to experiment not only with drugs, but also with different relationships without caring what other people thought about me.

One day I was eating lunch at school with a group of people and I told them I was frustrated with Tony and how he was treating me that day. I said I was tired of dealing with him and announced to the crowd, "I'm sick of guys; I just want to be a lesbian."

Out of nowhere, one girl in the group looked up at me and said, "Me, too."

I didn't think she was serious and she didn't think I was serious, but both of us *were* serious, and once we figured that out we gave it a shot and started dating. I was into sports and got along with guys better than I did with girls, so I felt like a boy sometimes and thought maybe I could be a little bit of a lesbian. Plus, I was curious and I'm an open person, so I thought, *Why not give it a try?* I could take a few weeks off from Tony and he wouldn't even notice.

She was cool, too. We got to know each other a little and started holding hands around school. We got so much attention for that; people would point and stare, and we loved it.

After school we would make out and fool around. She was a little girl, but she was crazy, and a total partier. We had a lot in common. One time we had a threesome with a guy and we both had a lot of fun.

We liked each other, but our relationship lasted only a few weeks because after the threesome I realized I missed guys. After we broke up I found out that she was hooking up with her ex-boyfriend behind my back the entire time. What the fuck was that about?

One guy who stepped in whenever I didn't like Tony for a week or I decided I wasn't a lesbian was Mark, who I secretly dated on and off through the beginning of high school. He was a tall black guy who looked exactly like Dave Chappelle. He was my baby, but our relationship was always on the down-low. After school, on days when Tony wasn't around, he and I would go around the corner, smoke a blunt, and go to his place and have sex. He had a good heart and the biggest penis in the whole world. The sex was great.

I took him to a couple of school dances, because Tony would never go, and people thought we were an odd couple—a short little blonde girl and a big-ass black guy—and even though we swore to everyone we were just friends, I loved him. Sadly, Mark died in a car accident in 2008. I'll always have a place in my heart for him, and looking back I wish I had gotten into a real relationship with him because instead of taking him seriously I spent more time with Tony, which was not a good move.

Whenever I'd meet up with Tony we'd go off somewhere and cause trouble. If his crew ran into another crew a fight would almost always break out. The guys loved to throw down. I wasn't into the drama, but at the same time, I'd rather be with the kids doing the punching than with the kids getting their faces bloodied.

Tony and I had been hanging out for a few months when one night we were walking down a side street to meet some friends at the park and all of a sudden cops showed up out of nowhere. It was like a scene from a movie. One second everything was calm and the next three cop cars with their lights blazing and sirens blasting cornered us in a parking lot.

I freaked. I had no clue what was going on, and put my hands up as the cops instructed.

Tony was a tough guy who never showed any emotion. I knew he had feelings for me even though he never acted like it. But at that moment, for one second, he had a heart. He turned to me and said, "You need to stay away from all this. You're better than this."

Those words ran through my brain in slow motion. I *was* better than this. He was right. While I was still processing what he said, he turned to me again and said, "Go have a good life," and bolted off.

The cops ran after him, leaving me in the parking lot all alone for a minute or two. Soon after, a cop came back and put me in his car. I heard on the radio that they caught Tony and that he pulled a knife on the cops before they wrestled him to the ground and cuffed him. I'm not a hundred percent sure what it was he was being picked up for, but the list of potential reasons is pretty endless. He went to jail for a while.

Inside the car, the cop and his partner were trying to get me to talk but I wouldn't. They were asking me who all of these people were, and I knew them all, but I didn't rat them out. We even drove by the house the group would hang out in and I wouldn't back down. Just like when my mom dragged me into juvenille hall, I didn't fear the authorities. But I did duck down when the cops drove past the house where all the kids hung out. Those people I was afraid of.

The cops eventually drove me home, told me I was too young to be out on the streets at that hour—there was a teen curfew at the time—and left me with my mom, who of course was furious. I had lied to her about where I was going that night in the first place, so coming home in the back of a cop car wasn't exactly what she was expecting.

I went back to the group's hangout spot a few months later and everyone in the house yelled at me and threatened to kick my ass. They thought I was a rat and had something to do with Tony getting arrested. I would never do that, and I told them so, but they didn't believe me. I didn't care. Tony was right: I was better than that.

———

*W*hile I knew I was better than that, my mom wasn't so convinced. She grounded me for what seemed like a lifetime.

I wasn't ready for that kind of punishment. Freshman year

was ending and there was no way I was going to spend my summer locked up in that house. So the night after Tony got arrested, I packed a bag and ran away. Of course, I went back to Brittany's house; this time my mom didn't come running for me. I still went to school enough days to finish the year with barely passing grades.

Brittany's family let me stay into the summer and they treated me really well, though I never asked them for anything. I felt bad even taking a shower at their house.

Hygiene was the least of my worries, anyway. Even though I was done hanging out with that crew of rough kids, I was still very heavy into crystal meth that summer. I could get it pretty easily; I was back hanging out with the guys from the apartment complex, and one of the guy's brothers who lived a block away always had crystal, so I had easy access.

I spent my days doing coke at the apartment and occasionally going to this guy's house to smoke meth. Sometimes I still hung out with Brittany, but plenty of times I was on my own, bouncing around from one place to another, doing as many drugs as I could get my hands on.

Despite my erratic behavior that summer I started dating my dream guy. He had just graduated and all year I had watched him hold hands with his girlfriend during school and sit in the grass eating lunch with her while I fantasized that he and I were sharing a tuna fish sandwich instead.

They broke up early that summer and we connected at a party in town.

He was a cute, blond-haired surfer who drove a little Volkswagen Beetle and spent his days at the beach perfecting his tan.

He was a really good guy and he treated me well. He'd pick me up from Brittany's house and take me on real dates. I didn't go with him to watch him beat people up or steal something from a quickie-mart. He was a gentleman, not a slimeball like most of the guys I'd been with, and I liked that. Plus, we looked really good together.

He smoked weed but didn't do any other drugs. A part of me wished I could be like that, but another side of me knew that weed wouldn't be enough.

When I wasn't with him I was out doing crystal or coke. He would pick me up from Brittany's or from some party and not realize I was on drugs. I didn't lie to him; he just never really asked. That worked out fine when I was staying at Brittany's house, but when her family went to Texas for a two-week summer vacation and I stayed with him and his dad, my habit became harder to hide.

Mr. Perfect worked at Outback Steakhouse, and when he was there I would use that free time to do more drugs. If he was working at night, I would go to a party and come home all messed up after he'd gone to sleep. I'd just sit in bed next to him, wired out of my mind, until the sun came up.

Eventually he either caught on or I chose drugs over him, because once Brittany came back to town our relationship was over. There wasn't a fight or anything; we were just looking for different things, so we went our separate ways. I didn't really care about the end of our relationship. I was always bouncing around and moving on from something, so this was just another opportunity for a new beginning for me.

What I didn't realize at the time was that I was in a very bad place. My first night back at Brittany's, I showed up high on crystal. Then I went days without sleeping. She knew I was in trouble, and she sat me down and tried to talk some sense into me.

"You look terrible," she said.

"I'm fine," I fired back defensively.

"Having fun every once in a while is one thing, but you are killing yourself."

"I know what I'm doing," I said. "Everything is *fine*."

She was worried. She'd go with me to parties and couldn't believe the amount of drugs I was doing. I was doing coke or crystal almost every day, and she was very scared for me, but her telling me to try to stop only made me want to do more drugs. I was spiraling out of control.

I was fucked up all the time and when I was coming down I got very depressed and angry. Drugs were no longer something I did for fun. The coke, weed, acid, crystal meth, alcohol, and whatever pills I could get my hands on kept my mind in a haze. They allowed me to not think, which I needed, because when I had time to think bad things happened.

In order to take away my internal pain, I created physical pain by cutting myself. One day it was boy trouble; another day I felt like I wanted to run away but had nowhere to go. I either felt like no one was looking out for me or that I had no one to turn to. I was alone and I was miserable.

I'd take scissors and jab them in my arm, slicing until a stream of blood ran down to my hand. With tears running down my face, I cut until I couldn't cut anymore. Then I'd decide to deal with my issues another way and do a line of coke. There seemed no end to the madness.

For weeks I kept cutting and hiding it from everyone. My arm was filled with gashes, but no one noticed. Then one day I had the scissors in my hand as I sat on Brittany's bedroom floor and she walked in and screamed at the top of her lungs. She grabbed the scissors out of my hand and, crying hysterically, wrapped her arms around me. She didn't know what to do, and I didn't know what to say. I was out of answers and excuses, and she was too scared to continue taking care of me.

It was time to go home.

My mom took me back, of course. She didn't really have a choice. I continued cutting, and she didn't know what to do, either.

I started becoming suicidal. One day I went through the medicine cabinet and took everything I could find. I put pill after pill in my mouth, but it wasn't enough. My mom and grandmother walked in on me as I was sitting on the bathroom floor surrounded by pill bottles and freaked out. They rushed me to the hospital, where the doctors said they were either going to pump my stomach or I could drink two cups of pure charcoal (I'm not really sure what that does, but I guess it works). I went with the charcoal, which was black and thick and tasted exactly how you would expect charcoal to taste. I gagged a bunch, but I kept it down.

Before I could leave the hospital I had to write a letter promising that I would never attempt suicide again and that if I ever had a problem I would talk to my mom instead of taking a bunch of pills. As you can imagine, that didn't work, so my mom forced me to go to counseling. I was open and told the counselor how I felt, but talking about my feelings didn't help. Hiding it didn't help, counseling didn't help—I just felt so lost. There were no answers.

I quickly went back to cutting whenever I was upset or high and crazy. It felt good. It was my way of dealing with all the teenage stress I had inside me. I always thought I was such an adult, but the truth was I couldn't handle being fifteen. Everything made me depressed, which in turn drove me to cut myself.

One day right after summer ended and I was back in school, I got called down to the nurse's office. I was nervous. Being called to the nurse's office was not common.

"Let me see your arm," she said when I walked in.

"No," I yelled, refusing to push up my long sleeves. Someone had clearly ratted me out, and I was mad.

"I need to see your arm."

"No!" I shouted again.

One of the counselors came in and held me down while the nurse lifted my sleeves. They saw the cut marks.

I had promised my mom I would stop. I had promised her I would straighten out.

I had lied.

On the school's recommendation, my mom picked me up and took me to Mesa Vista Hospital, a psychiatric ward in San Diego. For two weeks I stayed in the mental institution. I felt like a crazy person the entire time. While I was there I got into a fight and they put me in one of those white rooms with rubber walls. I was losing my mind. After that I was moved to another room, also with no windows. For two weeks I didn't see sunlight.

It's all kind of a blur to me now, but I remember being in there and my mom, grandma, grandpa, and brother visiting every few days. I was sad and wanted to go home, but I knew I had to stay. I knew I was sick.

I was still so depressed and cried a lot. Every night the nurses gave us antidepressant pills, and they would check our mouths to make sure we took them. The pills actually did more bad than good, I think. Considering I had a problem with pills to begin with, I thought I was better off without them. So I vowed that when I got out of there I would stop taking them on my own.

Some nights the nurses took us to Alcoholics Anonymous meetings. I was fifteen and I was sitting in a room full of adults in an AA meeting. I drank a lot back then, but that was the least of my problems. The counselors wanted us to see how we would end up if we continued using drugs, but for me the scare tactics didn't work.

I had two roommates at Mesa Vista. They didn't really care about me, and I didn't care about them. I was a lot more involved with drugs than most of the people around me; they all seemed to have their heads on straighter than I did.

We were allowed one phone call every two days and I used mine to talk to Brittany every time. She would tell me about the fun things she was doing or some party she'd just gone to. I wanted to be there with her. It seemed like all my friends were having fun without me, and knowing that made me cry.

I needed to get out of there. I tried to prove to the counselor that I was better so I could leave, but she started being a bitch so I lost my cool and cursed at her.

Mesa Vista was not helping me. I didn't think I needed to be there, and they couldn't help me—mainly because I wasn't ready to be helped. All I wanted was one line of coke. I wasn't addicted. I swear I wasn't. I didn't need coke, I just wanted it. I just wanted *anything* to make me better.

I wanted to escape life. I wanted to just run as far as I could run. I would've run to China, but I couldn't. I couldn't go anywhere. I felt like I was in prison, like I was trapped—not only at Mesa Vista, but in a pool of my own problems.

I heard somewhere that you could overdose on toothpaste, so one night I tried to eat an entire tube of toothpaste. It didn't work.

Nothing can describe my pain during that time more than the fact that I tried to overdose on toothpaste. That's as low as it gets.

Maybe I actually *was* an addict. Maybe I couldn't control myself. I don't know. Either way, I had a serious problem.

CHAPTER 7

Hitting Bottom

After two weeks of hell I left Mesa Vista and returned home pretty much the same as when I'd left. Being out in the real world was nice, though, and I started to feel a little better about myself and stopped having suicidal thoughts. I stopped cutting, too, which was good, but I was not ready to give up drugs.

I could see that my mom was still very worried about me. She looked like she hadn't slept in weeks. I felt terrible that I was putting her through so much, but that didn't stop me.

As soon as I got home I went right out to see my friends. Two weeks in Mesa Vista felt like a lifetime away from the apartment complex and all the parties. I missed being around my people and all the social aspects that go along with doing drugs—I needed to get right back into the swing of things. Almost everyone I hung out with was a druggie. Most of my friends didn't go to school. A lot of them had jobs making more than minimum wage. They didn't seem to have responsibilities or stress in their lives. Instead, every day was one big party.

My mom saw that I wasn't ready to grow up from that life just yet, so shortly after I returned from Mesa Vista she enrolled me in Sunset High School in Encinitas, which was a continuation school for kids who were on drugs or named Kendra. It had all the classes a regular school would have, but the day was also packed with hours of counseling.

These types of schools are really only good for kids who want to be there. At the end of the day, someone has to make the decision to get better on his or her own. I wasn't ready for that. Instead of taking it as an opportunity to get better I took it as a challenge to get more drugs. As it turned out, finding drugs wasn't hard at all. I was surrounded by druggies. Pretty much everyone had something on him or her at all times, and if they were afraid of getting caught they hid the drugs in the ceiling at the school. When the teacher left the room, we'd pop out the tiles of the drop ceiling and smoke weed or do lines of coke. Sometimes during lunch we would sneak out through a window when the teachers turned their backs, or go upstairs to the bathrooms to get high.

The whole day was dedicated to this game of seeing what we could get away with. Every conversation I had with the kids there was about drugs and how we were going to do them that day. There was a thrill to being bad and trying not to get caught.

The downside was that we were doing coke almost every day, which wasn't exactly what my mom had in mind when she sent me there.

We got drug-tested but we also took pills that flushed out our systems. It only worked some of the time, and I did get caught on a few occasions, but we never really got in trouble when we got busted. After all, we were already in reform school. Where else could they send us?

I knew the place was bad for me. I was doing drugs as often as possible and I could feel myself going crazy again. I told my mom that I wanted to go back to Clairemont. I told her that there were more drugs at this school than there were at my regular school. I begged her for another chance. She agreed and somehow convinced Clairemont High to take me back for my sophomore year.

Back in my old school, I almost immediately fell back into my old habits.

I started hanging out at the apartment complex where most of my troubles began. Some of the characters were still the same, but during my sophomore year I met a new guy. His name was Mario. He was Puerto Rican and very romantic. He had that Rico Suave thing going on but, more important, he always had drugs, so he immediately became part of our crew.

I was always just friends with the guys who hung out at the apartment complex. It was just a place to chill and get high; nothing romantic ever developed with any of them, and it was probably better that way. With Mario, though, things would be different.

I'm not sure exactly how it got started, but I think we were on acid that day. We hooked up and immediately began a relationship that would ultimately change my life. I started spending every day after school with Mario. Sometimes I would skip school, and all day long we'd do coke and have sex. Looking back I wouldn't call him my boyfriend. I never loved him. We just had a lot of sex and did a lot of coke.

Mario would give coke away to anyone and everyone who wanted it. It was pretty nuts. His parents were great people who lived in San Juan, but Mario had some local friends who definitely weren't so great.

At the time I wasn't concerned with any of that. I just loved hanging out with him. But since I was living at home I had to sneak around to make it happen.

Luckily my mom had a regular routine back then. She's still a creature of habit, but during that time especially you could keep time by her daily rituals. Every night at exactly nine o'clock she would go into the bathroom and brush her teeth, take off her makeup, and get ready for bed. From there she would crawl directly under the covers and call it a night.

Each night when I saw the bathroom light flick on I would sneak out of the house. I couldn't go out the front door because it made too much noise and it would have to stay locked, but we had a sliding glass door in the back that I could open quietly and sneak out, leaving it just a little bit open for when I came home. I would slowly creep out the back, hop over a big wall, and fall to the ground on the other side where a road led me to freedom—and to Mario. My legs would get all scraped up but I didn't care. I'd stay out all night, doing lots of coke and spending time with Mario.

Like clockwork, my mom was always up at six A.M., and five minutes later she would be in the shower. I'd sneak back through the sliding door while she was showering, put on my pajamas, crawl into bed, and pretend to be asleep. A few minutes later she'd get out of the shower and wake me up for school.

It worked every time.

I'd be a mess at school, of course, because I hadn't gotten any sleep the night before and was coming down off a night of heavy drug use. I would fall asleep in class and pass out on a bench during study hall or on the soccer field during PE. I was clearly in bad shape, but most people at school had already given up on me by that point so no one really cared.

One night, about a month into my routine, I snuck out at nine P.M. on the dot and spent the night getting messed up, as usual. But when I returned, the sliding glass door was locked.

My heart dropped. I didn't know what to do. I couldn't face my mom and the consequences that would follow, so I just went back to Mario's place and stayed there for a couple of days while I tried to figure things out.

The plan we eventually put together was terrible. I didn't have any clothes or money to buy new stuff, so I needed to go home and get my things. Even though I was only three or four months into my sophomore year of high school, I felt like I was an adult and ready to move out of my house.

Together, Mario and I marched over to my mom's house, knocked on the door, and told her I was moving out. I wasn't running away this time; I was packing my bags and leaving her, right in front of her face.

I could see the disappointment in her eyes. A part of her didn't believe it was happening, but another part of her knew there was nothing she could do to stop me. I felt bad, but I also felt like I was doing the right thing by leaving. It was time for me to be on my own.

We walked out the front door—no need to sneak out the back anymore—and I turned and said good-bye. She just let me go, and I really thought that was good-bye for good. I was starting a new life.

———

Moving in with Mario was not a good idea, to say the least. Deep down I knew that from the beginning, but I was never going to admit it.

I quit soccer and softball, then quit school altogether. Instead of going to high school like a normal fifteen-year-old, I sat in an apartment and did coke all day long.

Most days I didn't shower. I just rolled out of bed, went to the living room, and did a few lines. The coke mixed with a lack of funds led to me not eating very much, and I got really thin and became a scary-looking, smelly mess of a person.

Meanwhile, Mario was always talking about getting out of town and running away together to some luxurious place where we would be happy. But he was full of shit. He was never going anywhere. How could he?

During the day Mario worked in construction, but that didn't bring in enough money. Most of his funds came from selling drugs. At all hours of the day people would come in, usually without even knocking, to buy bags of coke from him. If Mario was at work it became my job to handle the drug sales.

Some really fucked up people would show up at the apartment, and each purchase was different. Some would want a gram; others would want an eight ball, which is about three and a half grams. I'd measure it out, put in a Baggie, and make the sale. Everyone paid and no one messed with me because people knew Mario was a tough guy and was not fucking around. It was like our life was straight out of a mafia movie: we were the reigning mafia couple and everyone knew to be afraid of us.

Whenever we were out of coke, we had to go see a guy who was high up the food chain in the drug-sales industry. He lived about fifteen miles away in the more upscale town of La Jolla, and his house was a real drug den, with lots of guns and scary people everywhere.

At one point Mario and I were in trouble because we weren't making enough money selling coke (probably because we were snorting all of the merchandise). We didn't have a TV and we were out of food so we had to go to the dealer and try to return the little bit of drugs we had in exchange for cash so we could live. Both of us were nervous, but we felt like we had no choice. We were like two crackheads heading over there, begging for a few dollars back. I don't remember if we ended up getting our money, but I lived to tell the story and at that point I guess that was good enough.

Just staying alive was a top priority during my time with Mario. I knew my limits with coke so usually I did a few lines and that was it. As much as I loved getting high, I was not trying to hurt myself. I was past my depressed and suicidal days and I wasn't going to go back to that dark place. However, I felt like I was alone in this new world, so I had to take care of myself. No one was going to jump in and save me. The whole time I was with Mario, I assumed my mom had given up on me, that she wasn't going to be there for me anymore. Years later I found out that she was at home worrying every second. She found out that Mario was selling drugs and she desperately wanted to get me out of there but she didn't know how. Worrying consumed her life, and she didn't eat or sleep pretty much the entire time.

She even reached out to my dad for help, and at one point he got Mario's number from my mom and called me at his house to tell me he missed me. He said he wanted to meet and catch up. It had been years since we had seen each other and I was suspicious, but for some reason I agreed to see him. I guess I was still hoping there was some way I could save our relationship and have a dad again.

We agreed to meet at the Pacific Beach Block Party, a huge street fair in San Diego where adults go to listen to music and get drunk and kids go to play games and eat street-fair food. Everyone went.

When the day arrived, Mario and I went to the street fair to meet my dad. We had decided to meet in front of a specific bar on a specific street at a specific time. Everything was all set up for the big reunion.

I was nervous because I didn't know what I would think of him or what he would think of me. I knew even the slightest inappropriate remark or action on his part would set me off, and I sort of felt like I was setting myself up for disappointment. But I went through with it anyway.

Mario and I got to the meeting spot and waited. At about

ten minutes past when we were supposed to meet, my dad still wasn't there. I started to get mad, but I continued to wait it out.

A few minutes later I saw him walking toward me. My heart was racing. I started to think about what I would say to him, and how I would react to whatever it was he was going to say to me.

He had told me he missed me over the phone, so maybe he had a whole big speech planned about how he wanted to be part of my life. Maybe he was going to try to be a good father.

He got closer, and I began shaking.

Then, just as he got within a few feet of us and I opened my mouth to say hello, he looked at me, walked right past, and headed down the street toward a friend of his. The bastard didn't even recognize his own daughter.

We might as well have been miles apart. We weren't father and daughter, we were two strangers.

I was pretty upset after that, so Mario got me drunk and tried to help me forget about everything. I survived. I always did. But my drug habit was turning into a nightmare pretty quickly, and one night soon after, I almost didn't survive.

Mario had a bunch of people over to his house and we were all doing lots of coke. Line after line, I just kept going. Like I said, I usually knew my limit and stopped myself when I hit it because even though I was a druggie I was still fearful of anything bad happening. But that night, for no real reason other than the fact that I just stopped caring about life, I threw caution to the wind and kept doing more and more.

Brittany was there, and she and some of our other friends were telling me to stop. I didn't want to listen. My nose started bleeding, but I just wiped the blood away and did another line. I was out of control. My eyes started rolling back in my head and everyone started freaking out.

Brittany screamed, "Oh my God!" but she was the only one who really cared about me.

I was shaking and choking on the blood that was dripping down the back of my throat. The group took me to the bathroom, put me in the tub, and ran the water, and I kept yelling, "I'm fine!"

I wasn't fine. I was in serious trouble. Everyone thought I was dying, but no one wanted to get in trouble so they didn't call an ambulance or take me to the hospital. Mario didn't even do anything to help me. He just left me in the tub.

Eventually I worked my way from the tub to the bedroom, where I recovered on my own. I still felt terrible, but the shaking and the bleeding stopped and my eyes were back where they were supposed to be. At one point, Mario walked in with a CD topped with a pile of coke.

"Feeling better?" he asked.

"Yeah, a little," I replied in a sick little girl's voice.

"Want some?" he asked, shoving the CD in my face.

I was so pissed that I slapped the CD out of his hand and sent the coke flying everywhere.

"What the fuck is wrong with you?" he yelled.

I was thinking the same thing.

After a day or two, when the drugs had completely worn off and I was able to think straight, I decided that I had had enough. All the rehabs and different schools never made a difference, but that night I'd almost had an out-of-body experience. I saw myself falling apart, nearing the end, and it wasn't what I wanted. I wasn't going to live like that anymore.

Something hit me and I sat in bed and screamed at the top of my lungs, releasing all the negative energy inside of me. I was done—for real this time. I knew I had to change my life.

Mario was already at work, so I put all of my stuff in a trash bag and on the way out I wrote on the little chalkboard that hung by the door, "Sorry I had to leave you. I will always love you."

That wasn't true—I never loved him. He represented a terrible time in my life, and I always remember him as being a part of that. But writing that I loved him seemed like the nice thing to do. As it turned out, Mario ended up getting married, starting a family, and getting his life together in a way that made even my mom happy for him when she heard the news. I guess once he found *true* love, Mario was able to put a stop to some nasty habits.

Even though I did a lot of drugs and stretched myself to the limit, I never felt like I couldn't stop at any time. I never felt like I *needed* drugs; I just really, really liked how I felt when I was high. There's a difference.

I was able to make the decision to stop using and actually follow through, and almost instantly I was a new person.

I felt so good about myself. The hard part would be convincing the rest of the world that I was turning things around.

I left with my garbage bag of crap, nervous to face my mom again. I had lied to her and promised to change so many times, but I'd never come through. How could I ask her for forgiveness again?

I decided to try a few other options first.

I called my dad's mother and asked to crash with her, but she shot me down. I think I even tried my dad, but that didn't pan out. Finally, I called my grandmother and explained the situation.

"Grandma, I took some bad drugs and I nearly died," I said tearfully. "I'm done. I want to turn things around."

She started crying.

"I want to come home," I said. "But I can't face Mom. I can't look at her."

She said she would talk to my mom and explain the situation and try her hardest to get the two of us back together.

"But even if I talk to her," she said, "you're going to have to be an adult and walk back here and apologize face-to-face."

I knew she was right, and that it was time to start playing by the rules.

CHAPTER 8

All Work and No Play

I was terrified to go back home. I had left that house a strong girl without a care in the world and I was returning a thin, run-down shadow of my former self. I got to the corner of my block and stopped.

My mom and grandmother were having a garage sale that day, and they were outside greeting customers. I stood on the corner for a few minutes and watched them. It was symbolic in a way—them getting rid of old their old garbage on the same day I was planning to return home and prove that I wasn't worthless.

I took a deep breath and walked toward the house. There was an awkward silence for a second after my mom first saw me.

"Hi," she finally said in a tone that was a mixture of anger and relief.

I fell to my knees. Crying, I begged for forgiveness and promised that I had changed. I had said it before, but this time I really meant it.

"I swear, Mom, it's different this time."

She looked at me on the ground—I must've looked like I was proposing marriage—and saw that I was for real. She said that I would have to get a job and follow every rule she could come up with and treat her and my grandmother with respect. I promised her I would, and I meant it with all my heart. She knew it and, just like that, I was home again.

Continuing with my plan for a new Kendra, I went back to my high school to enroll for my junior year. First, I had to meet with counselors at the school and give them the same promises that I made to my mom. I said I wouldn't skip school, I would try my hardest to get good grades, and I would graduate on time.

They gave me a second chance (actually, it was more like a fourth chance at that point) and after I completed an IQ test filled with puzzles and riddles, the counselors at the school decided that I had a learning disability and had to be put in special-ed classes. Maybe if someone had figured out that I had a learning disability earlier in my life I would have been in the right classes, would have gotten better grades, and would have been more encouraged to do well in school. When I was in regular classes, teachers would laugh at me, and I always felt stupid. I was afraid to ask questions and I would get mad and frustrated when I didn't understand something. Maybe I should have asked more questions. It's their job as teachers to answer, isn't it? If a kid wants to learn, they have to help. But I always felt like I was slowing everyone down, so I never said anything and instead just gave up.

There was no giving up this time, though. I walked into

that special-ed class after lunch and even though I was a little embarrassed, I knew I had to stick it out. There were kids with all sorts of disabilities in the class, but at the end of the day I fit in better there than anywhere else. I held my head high because I knew that I was back at school learning, and that was all that mattered.

I didn't care what people thought. *So what if I'm in the special class. What the fuck is anyone going to do about it?* I would say to myself as I walked through the hallways.

Half of my daily schedule, including history and science, consisted of special-ed classes, where I could ask all the questions I wanted. After a little while, I didn't even need to raise my hand anymore. The teachers took time to make sure everyone understood what was being taught, and they helped us if we needed it. They didn't laugh if I said I wanted to be a marine biologist or make me wear short skirts to get good grades. They were on my side, and I knew it. I loved learning, and it felt great to know I was doing well.

Making friends was another story. I was basically a loner. I hated the cliquey shit anyway, but I didn't fit in with the goody-goody kids (even though I was trying to be one), and I wasn't going anywhere near the druggies or thugs. Worst of all, my best friend Brittany was moved to a charter school, so even she couldn't help me out during the school day.

I was actually most comfortable with the kids in my special-ed classes. I had never judged anyone or thought people were cool or not cool by the way they looked or dressed, and the special-ed kids were all the same way.

I got back into sports and played soccer for the high school team. I tried to get back into softball, too, but that didn't work out as well. I'd played on the JV team in the beginning of high school and quit when I got into drugs, but now that I was better I thought for sure I would make the team. I did really well at tryouts and knew I was good enough to be on varsity or, at the very least, the JV squad. But when the coaches posted the lists of players, I hadn't made either team. I hadn't even made the practice squad! What I think—no, what I know—happened was that there were a lot of politics around the sports teams, and I didn't fit in with the girls or what they were trying to do. I didn't really fit into what *anyone* was trying to do. Even though I loved soccer and this time I was playing with a clear head, wherever I looked for friends—either in class or on the soccer team—I often came up unsuccessful.

While I wasn't into judging people, most kids' parents judged me. San Diego is a big city, but my community was like a small town unto itself, and everybody talked. All the parents knew my history. They had seen me at my worst. I was labeled the bad kid, and even though I was turning things around, nobody wanted their kids hanging out with me. I felt like I had something to prove, so I dedicated my time to school and, staying true to my promise to my mother, I got a job.

My first real job was at Papa John's Pizza. It was the worst damn job ever. I knew that jobs weren't meant to be fun—at least that's what my mom reminded me almost every day—but this was exceptionally bad. I flipped pizza, answered phones, worked the register, and made boxes, all while the management yelled at me and found other bitch work around the restaurant for me to do. I was running around doing everything, getting cuts on my hands from the boxes, while they sat in the management office and talked on the phone. It sucked, but I made a solid $6.50 an hour and I valued every penny. I loved getting that paycheck, no matter how little it was worth. I was never into fancy things—okay, maybe shoes—so I was a really good saver. I put every check right into the bank.

I wasn't perfect, though. I still smoked weed every now and then, but after what I had been through I figured that was nothing. Plus, to stay calm and get through the day at Papa John's, it was necessary.

One time I went to work really high. It was Super Bowl Sunday or some other huge pizza-delivery day, and we were swamped with orders. I was answering phones, flipping pizzas, and juggling a bunch of other tasks all at once. The amount of work mixed with the weed caused me to screw up a lot, and a customer called with a complaint. Of course I was the one who answered the phone.

"Um, excuse me, miss, but our pizza doesn't have any cheese on it," he told me.

Oops. Turns out I'd forgotten to put cheese on some of the pizzas. The customer and my manager were equally unhappy. As you can expect, I was still in a good mood.

For the most part, junior year was going really well for me, and then one day it got even better. When I wasn't working, studying, playing soccer, or being an all-around amazing daughter, I often went down to Mission Beach to hang out. One weekend I was there with a girlfriend, walking around on the beach and checking out men with muscles, when two guys pulled up next to us on their motorcycles. They did some smooth talking and eventually convinced us to go for a ride with them. I hopped on the back of a bike belonging to Zack, a blond-haired white boy, and cruised around the bay and Pacific Beach. I was nervous about trusting this complete stranger with my life, but he seemed to know what he was doing. There was also something special about him that I couldn't quite put my finger on. We had a spark between us, and it was a great feeling.

He was twenty years old at the time, so I told him I was an eighteen-year-old senior. Of course I was still sixteen, but who was counting?

After that day we started talking on the phone pretty regularly. He was a good guy; he didn't drink or smoke, and I loved that about him. My whole world before Zack was about doing drugs and seeing how fucked up I could get on any given day. For a long time I didn't care about school. I didn't care about *life*. And just when I was really turning things around, up rides Mr. Charming on his motorcycle.

It was fate.

When we officially started dating, Zack would pick me up from school every day on his motorcycle. I always thought that was cool. I never hung out with any of the kids in my school, so no one was going to blow my cover with the whole lying-about-my-age thing. Besides, at the time I felt like I was over high school. I had been through so much already that I couldn't really relate to the high school kids who were just starting to experiment with certain things.

Zack and I were perfect together, and even though I'd had my share of experiences, I considered this to be my first real relationship. We would go to his house after school, which was about ten minutes from where I lived. He lived with his parents, who were still together, and they were really nice people. They were a happy little family, and I liked that. It's what I wanted.

When my birthday rolled around in June, I had to tell Zack I was actually just turning seventeen. He was mad at first, but he got over it. We were in love, so he couldn't stay mad for too long.

My mom loved Zack. She saw that he was a good person, and that I was a better person around him. He also had a real job: he worked for his dad in a family business—and my mom liked that he wasn't just some bum without an income. I was allowed to do whatever I wanted with him because she trusted him and, more important, she trusted me again.

That summer Zack and I spent a lot of time together, taking trips to the beach and two-hour motorcycle rides to Universal Studios that would make our asses raw. We also went on a trip to Las Vegas with our families, where we did all the touristy things together and joked that when our families weren't looking we would run off to a wedding chapel and get married. Obviously we were kidding, but we both really thought that we *would* get married one day.

By the start of my senior year, everything was working out for me. I had a boyfriend. I had a great relationship with my mom and grandmother. I had a job—a crappy job, but a job nonetheless. My grades were good and I was actually moved out of special-ed classes and into regular classes with the smart kids. I had set a goal to turn my life around, and I was doing it.

*D*uring senior year, I basically lived with Zack. I still went to my mom's house all the time, but I spent most nights with him.

By that point I really needed a car. I had saved a good amount of money, but it wasn't enough to buy one. Well, it might have been enough for just any car, but I wanted a specific 1995 Mitsubishi Eclipse we found in Chula Vista for $4,000. It was my dream car.

I had gotten really into cars and racing over the past few months so I knew exactly what I wanted. This car was a souped-up stick shift, with all black exterior and white rims, and lowered like a race car. It was the coolest car ever, and because I was doing so well, my grandmother bought it for me. It was the single greatest thing anyone had ever done for me. After I stole from her, scared her half to death by running away, did drugs under her nose, and betrayed her trust, she still found it in her heart to not only forgive me but also to give me the gift of a lifetime. It was enough that she even agreed to talk to me again after all I had put her through; I couldn't have been more grateful for the car. I promised that she wouldn't regret it, that I would use the car to get to work, and that I'd graduate with good grades and make her proud.

I kept my promise for the most part, but I also used the car to go to local illegal street races. At that time in San Diego, street racing was the thing to do. I was finally a good kid, but I still needed some excitement.

Word would spread that a race would be taking place somewhere around town—there were four main spots where the races would go down—and everyone would gather at the spot, with their souped-up cars, between midnight and four A.M. I would always be there on weekends, sometimes with my Eclipse, which by that point had huge house speakers in the trunk so I could blast music wherever I went, but usually I went in Brittany's red Ford Mustang with her. It was just like *The Fast and the Furious*—there was a starter girl with a flag, and the races would go on until the cops came and everyone scrambled to get out of there.

I raced a little, but mostly I was just there to watch. My car didn't have an engine built for it, and my skills as a driver weren't really up for racing.

In fact, when I first got the car I didn't even know how to drive a stick. I had one of my racer friends come over and teach me how to drive. That day I had him drive us to a Denny's parking lot to practice. He was pulling around to the back of the restaurant when the driver in front of us forgot to put his car in drive and reversed right into my car. I jumped out and screamed like I have never screamed in my life. It sounded like someone was getting murdered. I was punching the ground and yelling at the top of my lungs, and people were holding me back because I was ready to kill the guy. I loved my car.

The driver paid to get it fixed, but all I wanted to do was show up at school in my new ride, and the next day I had to drive my damaged car into the parking lot. It wasn't exactly the moment of glory I had been looking forward to, but even with the dents I felt like a queen rolling up to school. It was still my dream car.

I continued to drive my awesome new car to school and to work every day, but after about a year and a half working at Papa John's, I'd had enough. I promised my grandmother I would continue to work, but I had to get out of there.

I started calling in sick all the time, and one day I just didn't show up to work. My boss called looking for me, and I told her I was done. She was pissed.

"You are worthless," she yelled. "You'll never work at another Papa John's again in your life."

"You are damn right I won't," I fired back.

I acted tough, but inside I was freaking out because I needed a job—not just because I'd promised my grandmother, but because I needed the money. I was saving so I could get my own place after graduation.

Luckily I had my senior project to keep me on a career path. At the beginning of the year we had to pick a career and spend the entire school year researching it, and at the end of the year we had to give a report on what we'd learned. The goal was to have us pick something we were interested in and then, hopefully, we'd work toward starting down the path to that career once graduation came.

I decided to do my project on registered nurses because my mom was working at an orthopedic center and I had easy access to nurses. Plus, my dreams of being a marine biologist had long since disappeared.

Working hard on the project but still in need of a paying job, I stumbled upon the career center at school one day. (I know, I was as shocked as anybody that I actually set foot in that place. I was a fun girl who still went to parties and races and stuff; I didn't do drugs anymore, but I was still not the career-center type.) I figured, *What the hell?* I went in and found an application to be an assistant at a dentist's office. The only requirement was that we had to be on a college path; the job would provide all the necessary training. It sounded cool so I applied, but a bunch of other students had applied as well, so I didn't really think much of it. When I got called in for an interview, I was shocked—and extremely nervous.

The interview was scheduled for after school, so the day I had to go for my meeting I went to school wearing one of my mom's sweaters, a nice skirt, and heels, and I did my hair. I looked so professional. I felt like every head was turning and looking at me as I walked through the hallways, and I loved it. Everyone was just stunned.

When I arrived for the interview I had to wait in the children's waiting room. I sat in a tiny chair, shaking, until the dentist was free to see me.

Just be yourself, I kept repeating in my head.

Eventually I calmed myself down and when I was called in I gave it my all. I went into the interview and wowed the dentist with my professionalism. He didn't see some girl who screwed up all the time. He saw someone with potential who knew how to speak and sit properly (my mom taught me that just before the interview). He thanked me for coming in and told me that I would be hearing from him soon.

I left that office with my head held high, feeling like I'd kicked some serious ass in there. A couple of days later the phone rang, and I found out I'd gotten the job. *Shut the fuck up!*

This was a real-ass job, and I was making nine dollars an hour. Suck on that, Papa John's! I was so proud of myself. They had interviewed kids from four different schools and probably had so many smarty-pants people walk in there, but they chose me, and I wasn't going to let them down.

I learned how to do everything at the dentist's office: the fluoride, the cleaning, the X-rays—anything a dental assistant with a degree would do. I asked tons of questions about teeth and the dentist really trained me well. I'd go in there with my gloves, all ready to work, and when I was done I'd run home and tell my mom about what I'd done that day. It really motivated me.

One time the father of a girl I played softball with came in to the office and I was told to put a crown on him. I thought, *Hell no!* I couldn't do that on a stranger, let alone someone I knew. Plus, he recognized me, so it was really awkward. But I'd been asked to do something, and it was my job, so I told him to open his mouth. My hands were shaking as I scraped along the inside of his gums to get all the shit off. I ended up putting the crown on, but I was way more comfortable teaching kids how to brush their teeth. That was my favorite part of the job—that and the paycheck, of course.

I was on top of the world. I had a boyfriend who loved me and a real job. I was doing well in school, and I was even in a television production class that I thought was fun and exciting. I did the morning announcements for the whole school and discovered I liked being in front of the camera.

When senior year came to a close I had to get up and give my senior project speech about being an RN. By that point I had been working at the dentist's office for a little while and no longer thought nursing was in the cards for me. I got up in front of the panel and starting discussing my research on nursing, and then I just stopped in the middle of my presentation.

"Listen," I said. "I starting doing this research on nursing, and then I got a job as an assistant at a dentist's office. Nursing is great, but I don't want to be a nurse. I go after school to this dental office where I . . ."

Then I just rambled on and on about all the great things I did at that job. I knew it was risky to ignore the rules and not read the paper I'd written on nursing, but I was getting real job experience.

" . . . So, in conclusion, I think I've learned a lot from this experience and I hope to someday be a dental hygienist," I finished.

After a brief awkward silence, the teachers clapped, and I passed. I was going to graduate. I had missed nearly a year and a half of school, but I made it. It was amazing.

My whole family came to my graduation ceremony. It was at Sea World, in the bird department, which was pretty cool. I wore a dress and little heels (which I still hated) and my hair was long and beautiful. It was a proud day, and my mom snapped a million photos. After all I had been through I had really beat the odds by graduating, and I felt like everyone there was happy for me. When they called my name and I walked onstage in my cap and gown it was the proudest moment of my life. It felt like everyone knew what I had gone through to get that diploma and was standing and cheering for me.

It was a shining moment, but there was one small problem: Without school to go to every day, what the hell was I supposed to do with my life?

CHAPTER 9

Working Hard for the Money

I really started to come into my own as a woman during that last year of high school. I wore makeup to school and began ditching the tomboy look. Being on camera for the television production class made me feel sexy—and so did going to car shows with Zack.

Toward the end of senior year and during the summer after graduation, Zack and I would head to car shows in Southern California to check out new and tricked-out, souped-up cars. We'd go alone, or sometimes with a group of his friends.

Since I was always more comfortable around guys than girls, I never really knew if I was sexy or not—and Zack's friends treated me like one of the boys. Being on TV at school had helped my self-image and allowed me to see that I was pretty, but I really didn't know how others saw me—and to be honest, I didn't really care all that much.

When we would go to car shows there would be girls modeling in front of cars and motorcycles, taking photos in company T-shirts and posing for different photographers. It seemed like a cool thing to do, but I never considered myself model material. Plus, I was there for the motorcycles, not the opportunity to be in pictures.

Then one day one of the motorcycle owners asked me to put on a T-shirt and pose for a few photos by his bike. I didn't really want to do it, but Zack talked me into it. I think he wanted his girlfriend to be like the other girls there so he could brag to his friends that he was dating a model.

"You are so sexy, baby," he said. "Just take a couple of photos."

So I put on the shirt, hopped on the bike, arranged my hair (which was down to my butt), and smiled for the photos. It was invigorating. I felt like a superstar, special and sexy.

I was hooked and Zack had a "that's my girl" look in his eyes, so I knew we would be going to car shows more often. Every time we returned I made sure I looked more and more sexy—I wore cutoff shorts, tight tops, and makeup—and the sexier I looked the more photographers wanted to shoot me. I even had people asking me for autographs. It was great.

It wasn't a job, though. It was just a fun way to boost my self-esteem every once in a while. Working a real job was becoming a problem; the dentist's office was starting to wear on me. I put in a good amount of time there and I was at a point where I couldn't really move up without more school, but the dentist was pushing me to fill crowns and use some of the sharp instruments that I wasn't comfortable using. I just wanted to help out and collect my paycheck, and he wanted me to be a dentist.

Plus, it was getting boring. I knew it wasn't going to work out much longer. Adding to my reasons for wanting to quit was the fact that Zack and I wanted to move out of his parents' house and into an apartment together, and I needed a bigger income to cover my end of the bills.

So, I needed money. I was feeling sexy because of the attention I was getting at the car shows. I was eighteen. I thought, *I should be a stripper.*

"Zack, I was thinking I could start to strip," I said confidently.

"No way."

"Look, it's really just dancing," I argued. "You know I can dance."

When I was in high school I was always dancing on tables and grinding on guys at parties. I would go to this all-ages club called Ice House and dance all night on the stage, hogging the spotlight and winning all sorts of ass-shaking contests. I was one of the only white girls up there, and I got a lot of respect for my ass-shaker. Clearly, I wasn't shy at all—I loved the attention, in fact.

"This is something I can do," I told Zack. "And I've been asking around, and I know I can make a lot of money for us."

"The money is good, but still—"

"Look, Zack, I love you," I said, turning on the charm. "This is all about the money. It'll be strictly business. I would never cheat on you."

"There are a lot of bad people in strip clubs."

"I'm tough," I assured him. "I can handle it."

I *was* tough. I wasn't going to let a guy do something that

I didn't want him to do, and I was totally dedicated to Zack. There would be no sex in the Champagne room for me.

"What about drugs?" he asked.

"You know I'm smarter than that. I'm done with that shit. I don't care what the other girls are doing; I'll never be some trashy, coke-whore stripper."

"I don't know . . ."

"Did I mention how much money we can make?"

He reluctantly agreed. I think he knew I was going to do it no matter what he said so he had no choice but to go along with my new plan.

I don't know where my new obsession with money came from, but as soon as I was out of school I developed the instinct to make as much as possible. If that meant stripping, then I could do that. I *would* do that. The next day I went down to Cheetah's, the most popular strip club in San Diego.

"Excuse me, sir, I would like to strip," I said to the owner. I was a nervous wreck, but I turned on the same professionalism that had landed me the job at the dentist's office. Of course, this time, instead of my mom's sweater I wore a tight little T-shirt and short cutoffs. I gave him my driver's license, and then I had to go downtown and get a stripper's license. (Yes, they have those. Who knew?) I filled out an application and took a picture for the license, and just like that I was a stripper.

Before my first night of work, I knew I had to go out and find something to make me look the part. All I really owned were cutoff shorts and a few old soccer uniforms. While some guys would probably find the uniform hot, I didn't think that was going to cut it at this club, so I went out and bought some stupid lingerie and big stripper boots. (Okay, I actually liked the boots.)

The night before my debut, I tried on the new outfit and stripped at home for Zack. He was impressed. My ass-shaking was top notch. I could be sexy, and he knew it. He'd always known it. Now I knew it, too.

I was very nervous on my first night. I didn't care so much about getting naked—I was comfortable being naked—but I was nervous about how the other girls would treat me, how the customers would treat me, if I was going to be any good at stripping.

Zack dropped me off and kissed me good-bye, and I walked into Cheetah's.

Walking into the club that first time was scary. It was dark and seemed overwhelmingly big. When my eyes adjusted, I saw a girl on the pole, naked and swinging around like a gymnast. I'm a pretty open person and I don't judge, but I hadn't seen the inside of a strip club at night before. I looked around and surveyed the scene. With the music blasting and the lights flashing, it was intense. I felt like a lost, shy little girl on the first day of school. *I'm going to do it*, I kept telling myself. *Don't back down.* I had to just keep thinking about the money.

I went into the dressing room to get changed and there were a bunch of girls already back there getting dolled up, talking about how they were doing that night.

"Hi, I'm Kendra," I said to the room. "I'm eighteen."

A couple of girls glanced over, then went right back to what they were doing—applying hair spray, using a curling iron, grabbing anything they could get their hands on to look pretty, smell pretty, and feel pretty enough to make the money.

"Can I sit here?" I said shyly to one girl as I made my way to the bench closest to the front. I didn't want to be in too deep. She looked kind of annoyed, and I felt like Forrest Gump when he gets on the school bus. *Seat's taken!*

Once I was dressed I went out to watch some of the girls in action. You get two songs on the stage—one to tease to and one to strip to. I watched as the girls worked the pole, teased the guys, and made their money. Then it was my turn: "Kendra to the main stage," blasted the MC's voice over the speakers.

I used my real name. Why not? What else was I going to use? I didn't think I looked like a Scarlett or a Maxine. I was Kendra, and that's what the customers were going to get.

I went onstage to a Limp Bizkit song and the crowd went wild. The owner didn't like hip-hop and I was into heavy metal that week anyway, so Limp Bizkit worked fine for me.

Doing the tease part seemed silly. I'm not a tease, so I stripped off all my clothes right away. The guys appreciated that. For the first time in my life I felt sexy, strong, confident, and powerful all at the same time. I was naked, free for the world to see, and I felt like the greatest person in the world. Dollar bills were flying everywhere, and I scooped them up as I danced.

When I was done one of the customers called me over. He was a thirtysomething average Joe white guy.

"Are you new here?" the obviously horny man who, rumor had it, was into the fresh meat at the club asked me.

"Yes, I am," I replied.

"Want to dance for me?"

So I gave him my very first lap dance. Actually, it was barely even a lap dance, since I didn't touch him at all—I wasn't sure what I was supposed to do or how close I was supposed to get. I didn't really want to go near him, but I didn't want to lose the job, either, so I just sort of danced around him and then sat and talked to him for a long time, which he seemed to like. You'd be surprised how many of the guys at strip clubs just want a girl to sit and talk and be flirty with them for a little while.

I danced a few sets, worked my way around the room, and talked to some more customers. By the end of the night the other girls were being really nice to me and had accepted me as one of them. They thought I was so little and cute; I guess it's hard to feel threatened by such a young, innocent-looking girl.

Before it was time to leave, my new friend, the fan of fresh meat, came over to me and handed me $2,000 in cash. I made more than two grand on my first night! He wanted me to "hang out" with him after my shift was over, but I told him "maybe next week"—a line I'd end up using with a lot of guys. There was no way that was ever happening, but I didn't want to lose the business.

I got a ride back to Zack's house as fast as I could. It was 4:30 in the morning when I got there, but I woke him up screaming.

"Look at what I got!" I yelled as I tossed the money onto the bed. "Two. Thousand. Dollars. In one night!"

Do you know how many pizzas I had to forget the cheese on or how many hours of teaching kids how to brush their teeth I needed to clock to make that kind of money? I felt like I had won the lottery, and all I had done was take my clothes off. How easy is that?

The next day Zack and I went and signed a lease on a new apartment. We used my $2,000 as a down payment for the first and last months' rent and a security deposit, and when it came time to fill out the application, under occupation I proudly wrote "stripper."

———

It wasn't long before I was completely comfortable at Cheetah's. I'd walk in with a big smile on my face and say hello to everyone. "What's up, girl?" I'd shout to a stripper friend who was grinding up on some customer. The other girls were like family to me.

After I'd say my hellos, I'd walk over to the DJ booth and check in, and then before I knew it they were playing my song. I started with Limp Bizkit, and my second song was Tim McGraw's "Something Like That" I loved country music, and that song was perfect:

I had a barbeque stain on my white T-shirt,
She was killing me in that miniskirt.

The crowd would go crazy.

Cheetah's was the most popular strip club in San Diego. The crowd was usually the same—younger people on the weekends and an older crowd during the week—and they had a lot of regulars, mostly white and Asian guys, and I got to know some of them really well.

The regulars just adored me, and that's why I made so much money. I know in the back rooms some girls will take it a little further than they are supposed to just to make some extra cash. Luckily, I never felt like I had to do that. I had a good group of guys who loved giving me their money so I made bank without having to cross any lines.

My feelings toward the customers wavered. On one hand, I always looked at the men as stupid; no matter what I was doing or saying to them, I was always thinking, *Give me my fucking money, you sucker.* I'd smile and say whatever it took to get them to just keep giving me more money. But then sometimes I would talk to them and I'd actually start considering them friends. I tried to be a tough bitch, but I'm also a softy.

One regular once told me that I would be famous someday. I thought, *Shut the fuck up!* It was like he was a fortune-teller or something, because the next words out of his mouth were, "You're going to be one of those famous girls at the Playboy Mansion."

"Are you just saying that because I'm giving you a lap dance right now?" I asked, laughing.

"No honey, for real," he said. "You're going to be famous."

For whatever reason, that stuck in my head.

Famous or not famous, I was the top earner at that strip club. Of course, I had slow nights where I would come home angry. I didn't want to strip for nothing! I was working my ass off out there, literally, so I wanted to get paid. Regardless of who made what, all the girls got along really well. We were happy for one another when someone was successful. It was a business for all of us; some girls had kids they were putting through school, and some were in school themselves. There were no crackheads in the bunch. By the end of my first night I was comfortable enough to walk into that locker room and sit wherever I wanted to sit and talk to whoever I wanted to talk to, and I didn't feel like a little girl in there anymore. After all, when you're stripping you grow up pretty fast.

One of the girls at the club and I got really close. We talked all the time, and eventually we started to get flirty with each other. When you work in a club where all of your coworkers are naked there is a pent-up sexual tension that you can't release. Sometimes I'd go home to Zack in the middle of the night and release it with him, but other times that wasn't an option.

This girl and I started talking about our past lesbian experiences, and the conversation got hot. Without saying it outright, we both knew where this talk was going. When I told her Zack was out of town, she let me know she was ready to party.

"Let me come over," she said, and after our shifts ended, we both went back to my place.

I had been down the girl-on-girl path before and it hadn't worked out, but I figured, hey, why not try it again? Once we were back at my place, we sat on the couch and had some drinks. Then she made the first move.

She leaned in and kissed me on the lips, then slowly moved down my neck. It was a little awkward but I was down. Eventually clothes started coming off and we were going at it. It was a fun night, but Zack was not happy about it when I told him what happened. "But it's a girl. How can you get mad?" I asked, but he and I could just not see eye-to-eye on the issue.

However, he got over it, and eventually we let her and a couple of others come over for threesomes on occasion. Okay, we never really had a threesome, because I never let Zack do anything with the other girls. I was allowed to have fun and do whatever I wanted, and he had to keep his eyes and hands on me. (That's fair, right?) Trust me, he wasn't too disappointed; I got a stripper pole for the house and put on private shows for him all the time.

Zack came to the club once in a while, but he wasn't really allowed to be there. Cheetah's, like many strip clubs, had a "no boyfriends" policy. At the end of the day, Zack didn't really care. I needed to work only one or two days a week, and I was coming home with tons of money. He actually quit his job and I started paying for everything. A friend of mine was living with us, too, and I supported her as well. Everyone was counting on me to be the moneymaker, so I kept at it. Every now and then I would have a bad night. Something crazy would happen at the club and I would get discouraged, but there was no turning back.

One night a teacher I'd had in high school showed up. I'd had him both freshman and senior years so he saw me at my worst and my best. He knew who I was and what I went through to turn my life around. Yes, I was stripping now, but I was a good person; I wasn't a hooker, I didn't do drugs, and I had a boyfriend I was probably going to marry. I thought I was doing pretty well, actually.

The teacher recognized me immediately. I looked at him and all I could think was *Oh my God, what are you doing here? That's so gross!* Within seconds of entering the club he walked up to me and said, "Hey, Kendra, do you know where I can get some blow?"

Gross!

"No," I told him. "I'm done with all that."

He was already completely fucked up and kept pushing. "Come on, I know you know," he said.

I was so mad. Who did this guy think he was? His dumb ass failed me once, too. What a fucked up asshole. I was so pissed off that I ran into the bathroom and hid from him the rest of the night.

That encounter really put things into perspective for me. That guy gave me a hard time in school and basically treated me like a failure, and a few years later he was in a strip club begging me for coke.

On another evening, Tony, my tagger jailbird boyfriend, walked into the club. I hadn't seen him since the cops took him that night and I'd thought I would never see him again. He'd gotten out of jail and heard I was working at Cheetah's so he decided to pop in.

"Remember me?" he asked.

Sex in the park, fighting constantly, cops driving me home after one of the scariest nights of my life—yeah, I remembered.

He sat for a while and watched me dance. I told him I had a boyfriend and eventually he just left. I didn't mind seeing him; it was like a blast from the past. Plus, it was nice to know he was still alive.

Other than a few odd nights, it was pretty smooth sailing at

Cheetah's, and I made good money. I clocked in and clocked out. It was all business.

Then one day Zack and I were in the car on the way to grab something to eat and I thought of an idea of how I could make business even better: bigger boobs!

Pamela Anderson was on the radio talking about saving animals or something, and all I could think about were her boobs. A lot of the customers at Cheetah's liked me because I *didn't* have big boobs—I was that innocent-looking girl guys always love. *But still*, I thought, *I'd do even better if I were bigger*. A lot of the girls had implants, and I felt like they would make me look and feel even sexier.

Just hearing Pam's voice was inspiration enough. The next time I was at the club I really studied the girls' breasts. I found the ones I liked the best and asked the owner of those perfect boobs for the number of her plastic surgeon. His name was Dr. Kim and I went up to L.A. for a consultation. Then I went back to San Diego, worked for two straight nights to collect my boob money, went back to L.A., and had them done.

I had my dream boobs and business was good!

CHAPTER 10

Adventure in Wonderland

$\mathcal{A}$fter about a year of stripping, taking care of Zack, and paying all the bills, Zack and I went to the car show where the photographer approached me about taking professional shots. I agreed to do them mainly for Zack. I wanted him to have the photos of me and always remember how beautiful I was. There were a lot of very attractive women at those car shows and at the parties we would go to, and I know Zack's eye wandered from time to time. But getting my boobs done and being told I was so beautiful every night at the strip club really boosted my confidence, so I felt good enough to take the photos.

I didn't take them thinking anything would come of it. Even when the photographer posted them on the modeling Web site, I thought little of it, so when those shots were discovered by *Playboy* and I was asked to work Hef's birthday party, I was shocked. (I was wearing my stripper clothes in those shots, by the way. It's not like *Playboy* saw me in sweatpants and decided they had to have me.)

The whole time leading up to that night at the Mansion, my family had no idea I was stripping. My mom thought Zack was working hard and paying for everything. In fact, she still thinks that, unless she is reading this book right now—in which case, sorry, Mom.

She did know about my new boobs, though. I went from a small B to a full C, so clearly she was going to notice at some point. All the other strippers freaked out when they saw them on me for the first time, so you can imagine what my mom's reaction would be when I told her: she was pissed! She said it was gross and trashy—and that was just over the phone when I broke the news. When I went home for Thanksgiving and she saw them for the first time, I could see the disappointment on her face. The boobs were new then and I was still really sore, but I refused to show any pain because the last thing I needed was an "I told you so" from her.

When I told her I was going to the Playboy Mansion she was even more upset. First, she didn't believe that it was Hef who had called me. She thought it was some sort of trick. Beyond that, she hated the idea of me going there. She tried desperately to keep me away from the Mansion and told me every *Playboy* rumor she could think of to try to scare me into not going.

"You know they have all these wild orgies there," she said. "Is that what you want to involve yourself in?"

The night of the party I knew my life was about to change. Nothing could have kept me from going. I've never been able to stay in one place for very long, and after nearly a year of living with Zack and stripping at Cheetah's, I knew I was ready for something new.

I still loved Zack, though. He was a good boyfriend. We got along really well, and sex with him was the best I'd ever had. I think when you are in a real relationship the sex is always better—you trust each other and open up in a way that you can't with some guy who sells you drugs or a guy who rips your clothes off in a park—and Zack and I were in love. Everything about our relationship was real, but being at the Playboy Mansion that night for Hef's birthday, I felt like something real was happening there, too.

That night was a lot of fun. Even though I wasn't supposed to drink on the job, I snuck Jell-O shots when no one was looking and got pretty buzzed. I saw Jack Nicholson and said hello and when he said "hi" back I totally freaked out. It was the coolest thing ever!

There were some awkward moments—like when an older couple approached me and told me they were swingers and asked me if I "wanted to have some fun"—but I wasn't going to let a few weirdos ruin my night. Everything was great once I ran into Tiffany Lang, a model I knew a little bit from San Diego. She was a painted girl, too, and had been at previous Mansion parties, so she showed me the ropes throughout the night. That was a huge relief because for the first time I actually felt young. When I was thirteen I wanted to hang out with twenty-year-olds—I was always that way—but that night at the Mansion, because I was out of my element I felt like a little girl. It showed me that there was room for me to grow and that there was a world outside San Diego that I needed to explore—and I felt like Hef was the guy who would help me with that.

After I left Hef that night, I walked down to the gates of the Mansion and met Zack, who was in his car waiting for me. Still covered in paint, I got in the passenger's seat and braced myself for the two-hour ride back to San Diego.

"So, how was it?" he asked with a hint of jealousy in his voice.

"It was fun," I told him. "I met a bunch of celebrities and served Jell-O shots, and that was really it."

"Did all the guys hit on you?"

"Not really, no."

"So, that's *really* it?"

"Well, Hugh Hefner asked me to be his girlfriend again," I said, nervously awaiting his reaction. "He wants me to come back to the Mansion this weekend for his real birthday."

Silence. Zack didn't say anything. He didn't think I was serious. He certainly didn't think Hef was for real. After a minute or two I changed the subject and we both brushed aside the *Playboy* talk. I didn't have much more to say on the subject.

I'd gotten paid a couple hundred dollars to work the party that evening, but the weekend invitation would be just for fun, a social call. I had always been focused on making money, so to take a weekend to go to the Playboy Mansion as a guest was a big leap—but it was a leap I decided I was ready to take.

A couple of days later Hef called and we worked out the details. He would send a car for me because at that point my

Eclipse had a few years on it and died all the time, and I didn't really trust it to get me all the way to Los Angeles.

When the weekend rolled around, I just split. I didn't bother going over the details with Zack again; I just hopped in the car and went.

A couple of hours later I was dropped off at the mansion and was soon totally lost. I was supposed to end up at the guesthouse, but I hadn't seen much more than the gym and the backyard the night of the party, so I had no idea where I was supposed to go. Plus, everything looked so different in the daylight. I felt like Alice after she falls down the rabbit hole—although this Wonderland was populated by hot, topless bunnies. Eventually a security guard found me and pointed me in the direction of the guesthouse, where all the Playmates stay.

I was assigned Room 2 of the guesthouse, and the second I walked in I jumped right on the bed. It was the comfiest bed I had ever lay on in my life. The room wasn't big, but something about it made it instantly feel like paradise.

Before arriving at the Mansion I had no idea what was planned for the weekend. I didn't know if I'd be in a bikini all weekend, or formalwear, or even painted again for that matter. As it turned out, there was going to be a big *Casablanca*-themed party that night, and that meant formalwear. Even my nicest pair of cutoff jeans was not going to cut it.

Bridget was the one who filled me in on the dress code. I slowly met her and some of the other girls throughout the day—usually if they came up and talked to me—and Bridget seemed to know the most about the weekend plans.

I didn't know what to do. The only formal affair I had ever been to was my prom, and I'd only stayed there for two minutes before leaving and changing into sweats.

I called Bridget—whose room number was on a list by my phone—for some help.

"Hi, this is Kendra," I said in slightly less of a little girl's voice than I would have once used. "I don't really know where I am right now or what I'm doing here, but I was told I need to be in a fancy dress tonight and I don't have one."

"I'll be right down," she replied sweetly.

Minutes later she showed up at my door, all dolled up in a black formal gown.

"Whoa, is that what I'm supposed to be wearing?" I asked.

"Of course, silly. It's *Casablanca* night."

I didn't know what to say. She took me to her room in the Mansion, which was all pink and super-girly. I thought it was cool, even though it wasn't necessarily my style. We went through her closet and found the perfect black dress for me to wear. Bridget was so nice, and she totally helped me out when she didn't even know me. I played with her cat for a little while, got dressed, and eventually went down for dinner.

We all sat down at the table—Hef and six or seven girls, including me—and I did my best to act like I belonged. It was a buffet-style meal and I watched how the other girls served themselves and then took exactly the same amount of food as they took. When we sat down I barely ate—I was too scared.

The whole time, Hef kept looking at me and giving me the eye, and it made me feel good that he even bothered to pay attention to me with so many other hot girls at the table. I also started enjoying the whole Mansion scene: butlers, comfy beds, good food—I knew I could get used to it.

After dinner we posed for some photos with Hef and watched *Casablanca* in the movie room. I had never seen a black-and-white movie before and I wasn't really into the film. To make matters worse, I had to pee so bad, but I thought it would be rude to get up. I was crammed in a tiny space on the floor with all the other girls, and there was no way to get up without being disruptive. Plus, it was Hef's favorite movie and everyone else seemed like they were into it, so I wanted to be respectful. As soon as the movie was over I ran to the bathroom.

The next night was club night. All the girls got dolled up and climbed into a big stretch Hummer limo, where we popped open Champagne for the drive to Hollywood. It was my first time in a limo, but I tried my hardest to act like I was used to it because no one else seemed to think it was amazing to be riding around in a huge-ass Hummer.

At the club we drank and danced. I did a little booty-shaking, and by the end of the night I was a little drunk and in a fun party mood.

On the ride home one of the girls asked me if I wanted to go upstairs into Hef's room with everyone once we got back to the Mansion. In my head I could hear my mom's voice: *You know they have orgies up there.* The alcohol had made me a little tipsy, but I was still out of my comfort zone. I didn't really believe the stories my mom told me—I thought it was all hype—but not knowing what to expect made me nervous.

"So do you want to come upstairs?" she asked again when we got back to the house.

Orgies. Orgies. Orgies.

"Okay, if I have to."

I didn't have to, obviously. I would never have to do anything at the Mansion that I didn't want to do. It seemed like every other girl was going up there, though, and that if I didn't go, too, it would be weird.

Before heading up, I went with a girl named Natalie to her room—the room that would one day become my room—and she instantly scared the crap out of me.

"Do you want to borrow panties?" she asked.

Orgies. Orgies Orgies. What? Why would I borrow panties? What was going on here?

There I was, in this girl's room in the Playboy Mansion—a room that had a stripper pole in it—and I was being asked if I wanted to borrow panties before going up to Hugh Hefner's room with a bunch of other girls. What a crazy world I was in all of a sudden! This was a far cry from Papa John's and school projects. But I wasn't about to chicken out now, so I put on the girl's underwear and went upstairs, nervous and shy but also a little curious to see what "upstairs" was all about.

I followed her to Hef's room, the same bedroom you'd see Hef and Holly in on *The Girls Next Door*. But that night it wasn't the relaxing, comfortable bedroom fans have grown to love. Instead, it was pitch black, with club music blasting and porn playing on the big screen. The whole scene was really strange to me—and I was a girl who thought she had seen pretty much everything.

Sticking close to Natalie, I saw there were a bunch of girls in the bathtub. Natalie jumped in. I took off the panties that I had just borrowed and hopped in, too. I followed whatever the other girls were doing, and I said nothing.

Eventually everyone got out of the tub and climbed onto Hef's bed, where he was lying on his back waiting. There were about seven other girls with me, and we were all naked. Someone handed me some body gel, but I had no idea what I was supposed to do with it, so I set it aside on the bed.

Holly got things started by getting Hef going, um, orally. Meanwhile, some of the other girls were slapping ass, getting all kinky, and yelling out all sorts of crazy things. I was scared—these girls were strangers to me. I just sat on the edge of the bed and watched. I wanted to be left alone and only do what I had to do.

One by one, each girl hopped on Hef and had sex with him. By this point my mom's voice was no longer in my head, thank goodness. I was just focused on what was going on in front of me.

Each girl rode Hef for about a minute or so and then hopped off and did her own thing—some fooled around with the other girls, while others just sort of sat to the side and watched. I studied their every move.

Then it was my turn.

I had been taking notes in my head, so I knew about a minute was all I needed to put in. Counting the time in my head, I had sex with Hef for the first time. At about the minute mark, I pulled away and it was done. It was like a job. Clock in, clock out. Or in this case, cock in, cock out.

I was definitely nervous up until that moment, but afterward I didn't really think too much of it. I was just going with the flow. I wasn't thinking about how much older Hef was—all the parts worked the same, even at his age; at the end of the day a body is a body. Plus, he was a successful, powerful, charming man, and those qualities pulled me right in. But it was still very weird.

It's not like I enjoyed having sex with him at the same time as all those other girls. I felt like I had to do it more than I wanted to do it. But I didn't have to be there. I *wanted* to be there. I *liked* being there. And if I had taken the time to weigh the pros and cons, I still would have done it. It's strange to look back on what I was thinking at the time. Hef's such a great friend and an important person in my life now, and our relationship seems so natural, but on that first night, I had no idea we would become as close as we are.

After the sex portion of the evening was over, the girls all got into pj's and did their own thing around the house. I went to the kitchen and starting chatting with the butlers. They seemed like the most down-to-earth people in the whole place, so I immediately bonded with them. Plus, they told me I could order whatever I wanted, which made me like them even more. I got a big-ass hamburger and chili cheese fries, and I was in heaven. I think they were surprised to see me eat so much, but it was a good way to end the night.

For the most part the whole evening was a lot of fun; seeing the big picture made the time in Hef's room seem like less of a big deal. The one negative to the whole *orgy, orgy, orgy* was thinking about Zack. I had never cheated on him before—with a guy, at least—and I didn't know where this would leave us.

I knew our relationship was probably ending, but I wasn't

really sure how I would explain myself to him. All I knew was that things were changing for me. This was about to become my new life. I could feel it. And with that thought in my head, I went to sleep.

The next morning Hef came into my room to see how I was doing. Hef *never* went in the guesthouse. I'd done my research on him, so I knew that.

"Hello, my darling," he said.

He was so charming. That was all it took to make the crazy thoughts that had been bouncing around my head the night before go away.

Hef didn't go to the other girls' rooms. He'd singled me out. I felt special, loved, and pretty. Isn't that all a girl really wants out of a boyfriend?

"Get your suit on," he said. "Everyone is in the pool."

We went down to the pool and swam and lay around in the sun all day. I enjoyed a beautiful day at a beautiful mansion and took it as a sign of a beautiful new beginning.

CHAPTER 11

Fresh Princess of Bel Air

After that weekend, I returned to Zack as a different girl. I felt like he and I were drifting apart, but I didn't think he saw it that way, and I was anxious to see how everything would play out.

When I got home, he asked me only basic questions about my weekend. "So how was it?" was about as detailed as he wanted to get, which was great, because "Fine" was really all the information I wanted to offer.

We mostly kept our distance and didn't talk about where I'd been or what I'd done. He didn't want to know, and I didn't want to tell him. Some things are better left unspoken.

Over the next five or six weeks I returned to the Mansion every weekend. Every Friday Hef would send the car, and every Sunday I would return to my life in San Diego. I'd been invited to move to the Mansion full-time, but I couldn't because during my first phone call with Hef I'd lied and told him I was in school. Mark had told me that Hef liked girls who were in college, so I'd told him what I thought he wanted to hear. Of course that meant I had to be "in school" during the week, until summer arrived, when I would be free to be at the Mansion full-time.

Meanwhile, I was spending my weekdays in San Diego waiting around for the weekend. I had nothing going on there anymore. I went into Cheetah's a couple of times just to pay the bills, but I was ready for a change.

When summer rolled around, I was out of excuses and ready to make the move. The only problem was that I still had a few months left on my apartment lease, and I had both Zack and a roommate counting on me to pay the bills.

"How much?" Hef asked when I told him my problem.

"What do you mean?"

"Well, if you can't move in and be my girlfriend until the lease is up, how much would it cost to just pay for it all right now?"

"I don't know, a little over four grand, maybe," I said, unsure of what he was going to do.

That weekend he came to my room at the guesthouse and handed me an envelope. Inside was $5,000 in cash. All I could do was smile. He liked me so much that he wasn't going to let a few months of rent stop me from moving into the Mansion. I was flattered. If I was wavering at all about what I wanted to do, this put my doubts to rest. I knew then that I would be moving to the Playboy Mansion full-time.

When I went back to Zack after that weekend, I sat him down, handed him the cash, and told him my plan.

"Hef wants me to move up there full-time," I said in the most serious voice I had ever used.

"Well, what about us?"

"We'll be fine," I assured him. "It will only be for a few months, and then I'll be back." I knew it would be longer, but I felt bad so I gave him something to hold on to.

"So we'll be back together when you come back?"

"Yes, I promise."

"Then why go? What's the point?" he asked.

"This could be good for me," I said. "It's a good place to be for a few months. I just feel like it's a good idea." I knew it was over with Zack. I was losing interest in him, but I didn't want to break his heart.

"Okay," he said. "If that's what you want."

"It is."

"I'll be here when you get back."

I packed a couple of suitcases and told Cheetah's that I was moving to the Playboy Mansion. They didn't seem to care very much.

With Zack, the good-bye was a little harder. He didn't know what was actually happening, but I knew this would be good-bye for good. When he realized I was taking my dogs, Raskal and Martini, Zack was not happy. I got them when we were together, so there definitely was some attachment there, but it's hard to say whether he wanted to keep the dogs or if he knew that my taking them meant I was probably not coming back. Either way, he was pissed off, and the good-bye felt more bitter and angry than anything else.

I hopped in the limo that Hef sent for me and took off. I

didn't bother saying good-bye to my mom. I knew she wasn't happy about the move, and after Zack's reaction I didn't want to hear it. There were no tears on my end; this was a happy occasion for me. I spent the whole two-hour ride looking out the window, and it felt like a spiritual event. *Where is this road taking me?* I thought. I knew moving to the Mansion was a risk, but I also knew that I had little to lose. In my gut I knew it was a good idea, but I worried a bit about what I was getting myself into.

During those two hours I thought about everything I had done in my life—the hell I'd put my mom through, the danger I had put my own life in. After a while, I knew this wasn't a risk I was taking; this was a path I was meant to be on. This was my future, and I was excited about it.

When I pulled up to the Mansion I looked down and realized that Martini, who wasn't spayed, had had her period all over the nice limo that Hef sent for me. Some would say that was a bad sign. I just thought a dog having its period all over a limo was funny. I wonder if Hef knows Bob Barker . . .

Inside the Mansion, once again I felt a little lost. By that point I knew my way around, but I didn't know what I was supposed to be doing there. Did the other girls have jobs? What was I supposed to do all day? It was all very confusing, and I didn't have any friends to help me figure it out.

Bridget was so nice to me that first weekend, but our relationship quickly went south when it became known that I was moving in full-time. Hef had recently kicked out a bunch of girls because they were bad and did a lot of things to piss him off. Plus, those girls didn't get along with Holly and Bridget, and from day one, Holly was in charge and Bridget was a close second in command. With four different rooms open, Hef asked me if I wanted to live in Room 2, which was Natalie's old room. That was fine with me; it was a pretty awesome room. When I told Bridget I was moving in there, she flipped out.

"Room two?" she said. "You can't move in Room two. That's going to be my scrapbooking room!"

Umm . . . what?

She wasn't super-jealous, but I could tell she wasn't happy. Obviously our relationship would change over time, but in the beginning, when I first moved in, both Bridget and Holly were very territorial. They'd put in their time, and if they wanted Room 2 for scrapbooking instead of a human being, then that's the way it was going to be.

At the time I thought that they were so stuckup and weird. They told me that they were celebrities and hadn't worn the same outfit twice in the past six months. I showed up to the Mansion with everything I owned—three shirts, three pairs of jeans, some cutoffs, and some stripper clothes. How was I going to not wear the same thing twice? I wore the same thing four days in a row. I still do! Deep down, I knew—well, I hoped— that I would somehow get along with Holly and Bridget. But I was never going to be like them.

I was really nervous. I was so different; I didn't see myself fitting in. I wasn't a celebrity—I was just some girl from Claremont. I couldn't compete with those girls. I instantly started questioning what I was doing there. I felt like I didn't belong. Plus, I had no money, so even if I *wanted* to look the way they looked, I could never afford to do so.

Somehow Hef heard about my situation and came to the rescue. He gave me $2,000 and sent Holly, Bridget, and me in a limo to the Beverly Center to find clothes for me. Even if the girls didn't like me, they loved shopping, so it was a good opportunity for us to spend time together. Maybe that was part of Hef's plan—I don't know—but I bought a bunch of clothes that Holly and Bridget liked on me and we had a great time. At the mall I bought a few tight things and some clothes that were just slightly nicer than my stripper clothes, and then we went to Melrose Avenue, where I got a bunch of sexy skirts. I looked at what Holly and Bridget were wearing and tried to find similar items. I realized what kind of girl Hef was looking for, and by the end of the day I had a closet full of clothes that made me one of the girls. I had also inched my way closer to having two friends in Holly and Bridget.

Even when they found out Hef had officially given me Room 2, they didn't complain. Not to me, at least. They just moved their scrapbooks somewhere else.

After shopping I was pooped, but I wanted to enjoy L.A. a little bit. I was hoping some of the girls would want to go out and have fun at a club or something, but when I asked around, I noticed most people were in their pajamas. I didn't understand what was going on, until someone told me we had a nine P.M. curfew.

What? Shut the fuck up!

My first day at the Mansion was overwhelming and exciting,

but my first night was one of the loneliest of my life. I used to strip until two in the morning. I was clearly a night person; I couldn't go to sleep at nine P.M. But that was the rule. Hef didn't want his girls out on the town, getting into trouble and hurting *Playboy*'s reputation.

That evening I sat in my room for a while, staring at the ceiling, not knowing what to do with myself. I took a bath in my new big Jacuzzi tub—soaking in my new life—and then went downstairs into the kitchen to talk to the butlers (even when I was just visiting, I always loved the butlers). I talked to them until two A.M. I wasn't sure what I was allowed to say or if I could ask about Hef and the other girls, so we just talked about sports and life. I also used that time to take advantage of the "eat anything you want" policy in the Mansion's kitchen. I had chili cheese fries and a cheeseburger and some beer. It was like a real-life *Willy Wonka and the Chocolate Factory*. I could have anything I wanted—and I did. I ate until I couldn't fit one more piece of food into my mouth. It was kind of gross, but delicious, too.

The next morning I woke up still full from my late-night meal but with nothing to do with my day. We had no responsibilities during most weekdays, so I sat around the house. I was so bored and felt so alone. I had Martini and Raskal there to keep me sane, but other than that I had no one.

The first time I visited the Mansion it seemed so big and overwhelming. I thought that I could stay there and be happy forever. After I'd lived there a couple weeks, the Mansion felt like home, and while it was still beautiful, it started to feel really small. I got used to my surroundings and I'd see the same people and feel like I was living in a tiny community instead of a big house. I would walk my dogs in the evening and have moments where I would look around, sigh, and try to take it all in because I knew early on that it wasn't going to last forever and I wanted to remember as much of the good parts of the experience as possible. Then at night it was back to the kitchen for more burgers and fries.

A few weeks after I moved into the Mansion, out of nowhere I was given a large amount of cash from Hef. As it turns out, I was supposed to get $1,000 a week as an allowance. I had no idea that was part of the deal when I moved in, but I was sure as hell happy to take it. I would have moved in regardless of the money, though; living in a Mansion with free food was enough for me.

I think Hef didn't mention the allowance because he doesn't want girls to move in for the money; he wants us to move in for him. And I did. Hef had already done so much for me—buying me clothes, paying off my rent—that I was never going to ask for money. Just like when I was a kid, I hated asking for money as an adult. But having the money was a nice bonus. Now I could finally live a little.

I started going out during the day and enjoying Los Angeles. I met a few Playmates and actually made a few friends. Slowly, I started getting used to the whole lifestyle.

At night, though, I would be in my pj's by nine P.M. and usually in the kitchen by nine thirty for burgers, cheese fries, and a stomachache—in that order.

It was a depressing routine and it got even worse when I started to gain weight. When you eat that garbage every night and lie around all day, it's bound to happen. After six months living there I had put on a good fifteen pounds and my confidence was at an all-time low.

It was tough to deal with the fact that I was gaining weight, and being surrounded by beautiful girls every day didn't help. Plus, every week we would get photos of ourselves that had been taken the one night a week we all went to the club or to a *Playboy* event, so I could look at the photos and see myself getting fatter from week to week.

One night we were all in the limo on the way to a book signing with Hef when he pulled me aside.

"Is everything okay?" he asked.

"I feel fat, Hef," I told him. "Everyone is so pretty. It's making me really insecure."

"Well, you look a little bigger," he said honestly. "Maybe you can go to the gym."

When we got home I went to my room and cried myself to sleep. I was so disappointed in myself. I had this whole Mansion and a great life to enjoy and all I was doing was lying around and eating. I felt so lazy and miserable. This was supposed to be paradise, but for me, it wasn't. Don't get me wrong, the parties were great, but every time they ended I would go back to feeling alone and lost. I guess there is a fine line between happy and sad—and on that line is a big plate of chili cheese fries.

CHAPTER 12

Party Hopping with Bunnies

 month in, I was really on the fence about whether I should stay at the Playboy Mansion. Yes, I had new clothes and a weekly allowance, but I was also bored to death and gaining weight by the second. I didn't know how much more I could take.

My mom, who was against me moving there in the first place, changed her mind about *Playboy* once I was settled. She hates change, and if it were up to her I would never try anything new, but shortly after I moved in she and my grandmother came to the Mansion to visit, and she quickly fell in love with my new life. Hef took us all out to a nice steak dinner and treated my mom and my grandmother like family. They all instantly bonded, and my mom saw not only the kind of life I was now living but also the great man I was living with.

From that visit on she considered the Mansion a place I should stay the rest of my life—not just for the money, but for the comfortable family environment it provided. So, when

I called her complaining and told her I might move back home, she fought me on it.

"Where would you be if you weren't there?" she asked. "Papa John's?"

It was tough love, but it was what I needed. Mom was right. It was time to make the best of the situation. This was the freakin' Playboy Mansion, after all. I needed to start having some fun. So I decided to whip my ass in shape, both mentally and physically.

I began playing in a softball league—at first with some of the people who worked at *Playboy*, and then later with random teams. I missed playing sports, and this was a good way for me to get in shape and have some "me" time. Plus it was cool to come back to the Mansion with my knees all bloodied and have everyone ask me what happened. I also started going to the gym and really working off those chili cheese fries.

I did my best to get out more and make friends with some of the other girls in the house and in the Playmate guesthouse. Some girls were great. I quickly bonded with Destiny Davis, a 2005 Playmate. We both loved hip-hop, and we were alike in so many ways. We called each other PIC because we were partners in crime—two ghetto white chicks always looking for fun. Then there was Tiffany Fallon, the 2005 Playmate of the Year, who was the one girl I saw as a role model at that place. She was classy, polite, always smiling, and constantly doing things to make *Playboy* look good. She was a real inspiration and a great friend.

I also got close to Carmella DeCesare, who, like me, loved sports, and was a really down-to-earth chick. She's married to quarterback Jeff Garcia, so of course she followed football, but she also loved basketball. During the Playmate of the Year dinner—an annual formal dinner, which that year honored Sara Underwood as the magazine's top centerfold—Carmella and I were more interested in the Lakers playoff game than the dinner. I wore a Lakers jersey to a fancy restaurant and all the girls angrily talked behind my back about how disrespectful I was. But the playoffs were more important to me, and Carmella and I kept getting up to check the score in the bar. I knew we would be friends from that day forward.

These girls, and some of the other Playmates, were really cool. We'd stay up until four A.M. laughing and having a great time, and then we'd go into the kitchen and hang with the butlers.

Bryant, DeAndre, Carlena, and some of the chefs were like my best friends. They were real people, and I liked that. At first we kept our conversations to general topics, but once they got to know me I opened up to them about all of my concerns about the Mansion. None of them thought I would last, but they were always there to hug me and stay up until five in the morning to listen to me whine about my problems. We had to be sneaky, though, because the staff wasn't really allowed to fraternize with the girlfriends. I think in the past girls had been caught sleeping with some of the staff, so Hef kept them off-limits after hours. On the rare occasion when Hef left his room late at night, the butlers or chefs would hear Hef's slippers shuffling across the floor and scatter and hide. Hef would walk into the kitchen and I'd be standing there by myself.

Even with the staff to entertain me, nights were hard because while my Playmate friends got to go out and party, I would have to be home by nine P.M. I'd get a text message from a girl that read, "Having so much fun in Vegas. Wish you were here! Partying with all these football players," and that was devastating. I felt so trapped and angry when I was missing out on something good.

However, sometimes when I would get out of the house, I would end up in bad situations with Playmates who were up to no good. One of those girls was former Miss United States Teen Kari Ann Peniche, who was staying at the Mansion for a few weeks while she shot a spread for the magazine.

Most of the girls at the Mansion were good girls, but Kari Ann had a different agenda. Her IMDB credits currently include *Celebrity Rehab with Dr. Drew* and a sex tape with Rebecca Gayheart and Eric Dane, but at the time I didn't know anything about her and I thought we could be friends. She seemed to know everyone in L.A., and all the fun places to hang out.

One day we were driving around Beverly Hills and she said she wanted to stop at her friend's house. We pulled up to a big apartment building on Doheny Drive and made our way to the unit where her "friend" lived. We rang the bell and an older guy answered the door and invited us inside. Although I thought he was a little weird, I just went along with it. Then he broke out a plate of cocaine.

Oh, no! I thought. *This isn't good.*

I felt very uncomfortable. I had been clean for so long and since then had never really been tempted to do real drugs. There was a stripper at Cheetah's who I was friends with who did coke, but for some reason it was easy to say no back then.

This time felt different. I was so far removed from the whole drug scene. I really had moved on in life. I smoked weed from time to time, but that didn't count. This was serious, and I was nervous.

Without the slightest hesitation, Kari Ann leaned over and did a line. Then she asked me if I wanted some. *What's one time really going to do to me?* I thought.

So I did it. I leaned over and snorted a line of cocaine. For the first minute or two it was the best damn feeling in the world. So much time had passed that I'd almost forgotten how it felt—it was amazing.

"This is some of the best shit," Kari Ann said.

I agreed, but when we left and I got in the car, I started getting paranoid. All these bad moments from my past started running through my head, and I started bugging out.

"What did I do?" I asked Kari Ann.

"Isn't it great?" she said.

"No, but I used to do it and—"

"Don't worry," she said. "It's pure stuff. You won't get addicted. Nothing is going to happen to you."

"But you don't understand . . ."

I didn't bother explaining. What was I going to do, tell her my whole life story? She wasn't going to understand.

We went to SkyBar at the Mondrian Hotel on the Sunset Strip and I was miserable. I felt so fucked up. The night finally ended and I tried to block it out of my mind. I knew I'd made a mistake, and I was never going to do it again. I just wanted to forget about it and move on.

For Kari Ann, it was a different story. Somehow word got

out that she had coke around the Mansion, and eventually the news made its way to Hef. I'm not sure who ratted her out, but drugs were a big no-no at the Mansion. Hef was very strict about it. He was a big supporter of legalized weed, but when it came to coke and other drugs he wouldn't stand for it. It was bad for *Playboy*'s image. Holly and Bridget were against it, too. They were real goody-goodies, and I think that's why Hef trusted them so much.

I, on the other hand, was always right on the edge of going off and doing something bad. The only way for me to survive was to cut Kari Ann out of my life completely. Later, when Hef had whatever confirmation he was looking for, he called Kari Ann into his office and told her she had to leave.

I was happy that she was leaving. But my involvement with her wasn't over just yet. Everyone knew that she and I had become friends and I started to worry that Hef or the girls would connect the two of us and think I was doing drugs, too. People seemed to know everything about everyone at the Mansion, and I was sure Holly and Bridget knew I'd done coke with Kari Ann that day.

Soon after Kari Ann left, Mary O'Connor, Hef's personal secretary, called me into her office and started asking me questions about her. They wanted to know if I was still talking to or texting her. She had been texting me, but I always ignored her. Normally I would stand up for a friend, but with Kari Ann, I understood. They didn't want her near anyone involved with *Playboy*. Her departure was the best thing that could've happened to me, because if she had hung around I'm sure I would have been tempted to do coke again.

Kari Ann wasn't the only crazy one hanging around at the Mansion, though.

There was also a Playmate from Atlanta, and when she came to the Mansion I thought she was so beautiful, and she seemed like a fun girl. We ended up going out one evening, again to SkyBar, and everything was fine. I was drinking, and there was no sign of drugs.

We were supposed to go to The Improv comedy club on Melrose Avenue for the night; we'd told the staff at the Mansion that's what we were doing, and I wanted to stick to the plan in case someone came to check up on us (which was always a possibility).

I don't know if she drank too much or was on something else, but all of a sudden she began grinding up on this random nasty-looking, blond-haired dude. Meanwhile, I just stood by myself at SkyBar counting the minutes until we had to leave for the comedy club.

Eventually she came up to me and gave me some bogus story about how the guy didn't have a ride home, and she asked if we could take him. I tried to say no but she kept insisting. We drove him to a house all the way up in the Hollywood Hills, and when we arrived she got out of the car and went inside with him, leaving me outside alone. *What the fuck?*

After about twenty minutes I went inside the house and started shouting her name and looking all over for her. I wanted to get to the comedy club, and I was sick of waiting. I opened a door to one of the rooms, and there she was with the guy, butt ass naked and doing lines of coke.

I yelled that it was time to go. Looking a little drugged-up and out of sorts, she got dressed and we went to the comedy club without the guy. A few years earlier, I probably would have stripped down and joined them—but not anymore. I just wanted to get to that comedy club and fucking laugh before I got even madder.

Of course once we arrived, she started falling all over the place, hitting on every guy there, and was just a completely gross mess. That chick was out of control. I'm not sure how she eventually ended things with Hef, but a few years later I heard she was arrested for cocaine possession.

Girls like these really made me skeptical about the people at the Mansion. I had a hard time figuring out who was good and who was bad, so after trying to make friends for a while and getting burned, I just sort of shut down and started living in my own world and keeping to myself.

I still didn't really have much of a relationship with Holly or Bridget at that point. We didn't have a lot in common, so we tended to go our separate ways. The two of them would spend some time together, but I was rarely invited to be part of their fun. Maybe they didn't like me back then; maybe they saw me as a threat, or maybe I was just not enough like them, but either way we were hardly friends.

Of course, when it was club night, we would all go out and then end up in the tub together before all taking turns with Hef in his bedroom. But even there we had no relationship. You'd think three girls who spent their Saturday nights together naked in a bathtub would find something to talk about during the week, but not us. When we were in that room with Hef we each did our own thing, and it was like the other girls weren't there. I usually got very drunk as I sat around waiting for my turn to do what I had to do. Then it was in and out and I was out of there. Very few words were said.

The best times in Hef's room were actually when other girls came up with us. Whenever there was a hot Playmate in the room, I would always have a good time. It brought more life to the party. I would be belligerent and act like a total fool, but the girl and I would usually mess around, smoke some weed, and kiss a little. That was fun. Bridget, Holly, and I had a different relationship; we never touched one another.

One time a crazy Russian chick came upstairs with us, and she was totally wild and kinky. She literally attacked me up there. Everyone was having a good time and out of nowhere she just bit me. I was like, "Bitch, get off!" She was insane, but most of the girls were fun.

That first night we went to Hef's room, when I didn't know anyone or anything about what was going to happen, I was scared, but as time went on I didn't care as much. There was always a fear of diseases, though. After that first time I ran to the doctor to get checked out and came back with a clean bill of health. Then as I got more comfortable in the Mansion I asked around about some of the new girls and it seemed like everyone was clean. I still got checked every few months, however, and in the back of my head there was always that fear. But since I was usually very, very drunk during those evenings, I tended not to care so much until the next day. I *had* to be very drunk or smoke lots of weed to survive those nights—there was no way around it.

I would spend the Sunday after club night hungover, and by

Monday I would be recovered enough to get back to sitting on my ass. The rest of the week would be okay, but the cycle was taking its toll on me and getting boring. I had to get out.

Instead of finding Playmates to hang out with, I decided I wanted to go to school. After all those years of skipping class and being forced to go to different schools because of my terrible behavior, I was actually deciding on my own that I wanted to enroll and apply myself. It's amazing how things can change over time.

I wasn't really sure what I wanted to go to school for, but I knew I had to get involved in something. I looked online at different options and came up with physical therapy classes at Bryman College. Hef was very supportive. He always wanted us learning and experiencing new things, so he paid for the entire program.

I loved school. I went for a few hours every day. I spent half the time massaging a person in class, and the rest of the time I learned about the anatomy of the human body, CPR, and various types of massaging techniques.

It was fun and interesting, but more important, it got me out of bed. I was up by 6:30 A.M. and in class by 7:30 A.M. every morning. Sure, I was late a lot for various reasons (I always found a way to get away with it), but still, I was there, which was pretty impressive considering we were going to the clubs with Hef two nights a week and staying up until three A.M. most nights. I was exhausted but I went to class.

I had my share of mishaps at school, of course. One day after I had been constipated for about five days, I took a laxative the night before class. It was the first time I'd ever taken one—I had never even heard of such a thing before—and I was told that it should work in three or four hours. The next morning I woke up and still nothing was happening down there. Then, about halfway through class, it hit me like a ton of bricks. I had to shit so bad, and the bathroom was practically in the classroom— it was set up like an elementary school, so the bathroom was tucked into a corner and not down the hall or far, far away, as I had hoped.

"I have to poop!" I announced to the class, and I ran to take care of my business. It was so gross. I was in there for about an hour and stunk up the whole classroom. I even made a sign once I got out that read DO NOT GO IN THERE and taped it to the bathroom door.

As if that wasn't bad enough, on my ride home from class I got a second stomachache. I drove back to the Mansion at approximately 105 miles per hour, and if a cop had come after me I wouldn't have pulled over. I flew west on I-10 and up the 405 North, weaving in and out of L.A. traffic, and made it back to the Mansion just in time to avoid shitting my pants.

While that was a rough day, school as a whole was definitely not shitty. It forced me to wake up early, it gave me my own thing to care about, and it made me start feeling good about myself again. It also kept me at the Playboy Mansion during a time when I was definitely thinking about leaving, which shortly after turned out to be a very good thing.

CHAPTER 13

Playing the Role of Kendra Wilkinson

Taking classes was the best decision I ever made at the Mansion. It gave my life some meaning and allowed me to start enjoying the incredible opportunity I'd been given. I mean, it's not every day that you get asked to live in the Playboy Mansion. I liked the parties and hanging out with Hef and everything else the Mansion had to offer, but school made me feel like I was doing something with my life, and that was important.

After school I continued to work out to get myself back into my pre-all-you-can-eat shape. I worked out like a maniac; I took martial arts classes at the Mansion, hiked Runyon Canyon regularly, and climbed the stairs in Santa Monica—a set of nearly two hundred steps that locals use for a workout. (At my best I could do the fifteen sets of stairs, which is pretty damn good.) I even took tennis lessons and played tennis with Ray Anthony, the inventor of "The Bunny Hop," and some of Hef's other friends. I *loved* Hef's friends. I thought Walter Ralph, the heir to the Ralph's grocery company, was the biggest celebrity ever. I'd hang out with all of Hef's buddies after movie nights, teaching them slang terms and getting these old guys to say things like "What it is, ho" to girls at parties.

Thanks to all the work I was putting in, I got in really good shape. I was going to sleep at normal hours, waking up early, and doing something with my days. I felt great, and with the workouts I was looking great, too. It's not easy to have high self-esteem when you're surrounded by all the hot-ass girls walking around that mansion. For a long time I compared myself to everyone else and nearly lost my mind because I felt like I couldn't compete. But with school on and the flab gone, my confidence was back to normal.

Soon after I'd declared victory over the chili cheese fries Hef came to us and said they were going to be filming a documentary at the Mansion. At the time I didn't know who "they" were, but eventually I found out it was producer Kevin Burns and his team. The film was going to be called *Holmby Hills*, after the area of Los Angeles where the Mansion is located, and it was going to be about Hef and his family. It seemed like a good idea for a documentary, but I wasn't sure at the time how—or even if—the other girls and I were going to be involved.

Somewhere along the line, the concept changed and it was decided that the documentary was going to be a reality show about Hef and his girls. We were all weirded out by that idea. Where were they going to film? How were they going to make us look? Holly, Bridget, and I didn't like it at all, and initially we all said no.

Despite the fact that we were very skeptical, we ended up

going along with it anyway. Hef wanted to do it, and I could have said no if I really didn't want to be on the show, but we trusted Hef and knew he wouldn't steer us in the wrong direction. Plus, I was just starting to really enjoy my time at the Mansion so I wasn't going to just pick up and leave over something like a little reality show.

A week or two later the camera crew came and shot the pilot, which was called "The Girls Next Door." They filmed me at therapy school for that episode. I was about to graduate and classes were over, but they liked the idea of me being in school so we rented out a chiropractic office for the day and filmed a pretend therapy school class with some friends of mine playing the roles of the teacher and students. It was so weird to me because it was supposed to be a *reality* show, and I assumed it would all be real, but instead the pilot was sort of just *based* on reality.

After the school scene, the producers sat me down and I did a twenty-minute interview on camera in which I talked about Hef and the Mansion and everything we do as girlfriends. I was wearing my Terrell Owens jersey because I was a die-hard TO fan and they wanted us wearing clothing that represented who we were.

Everything was going smoothly until the producers told us that they wanted to film us in Hef's room, where the action happened after club nights. When I heard that, I was pissed. There was no way they were filming me in there, or even walking in that room implying anything was going to happen. I was prepared to take a stand.

Holly, Bridget, and I talked it over even though we weren't

very close at the time. We knew we would have to stick together on this issue or we would get pushed around. I started getting aggressive about it and really rallied the girls into fighting for our privacy. Eventually, we agreed that our personal lives (which obviously included nights with Hef) should remain personal and we wouldn't be filmed anywhere near the room. We went to Hef and he agreed and told the producers that it wasn't going to happen.

Even with that win under our belts, the three of us were still very nervous about the show. We didn't know how they would portray us or how people who didn't know us would view us. But all the people behind the show loved it, so we were moving forward. Well, Bridget and Holly were moving forward. I soon realized the girls had other plans for me.

Even though we'd banded together to preserve our privacy, I still wasn't that close with them then, and by that point they were best friends. Since I wasn't fitting in to their little group, they thought the show might be better with another girl instead of with me. So Holly and Bridget went to Mary and told her that I was dating another guy behind Hef's back.

After living in the Mansion for a year I *did* miss dating, and there were times when I was out during the day (before my nine P.M. curfew) or at therapy school or even at *Playboy* parties when I met guys. It's only natural. I needed to have my own life or I would have gone crazy. But at the same time, I didn't want to disrespect Hef or the *Playboy* name—that always came first. So if I did meet someone, I kept it a big secret and made sure, especially when the show was filming, not to be photographed with them.

So yes, there was some truth to what they told Mary, but they weren't looking out for Hef's best interests. They just wanted me off the show. Instead of me, Holly and Bridget wanted to bring in Audra, this girl who was looking to move into the Mansion and become Hef's girlfriend. She and I had issues—our personalities totally clashed—and she was trying desperately to take my place, and for some reason Holly and Bridget were on her side. They all had a pact that they were going to stick together and get rid of me. I don't know why; I hadn't done anything wrong. I'm tough and I would never in a million years have let them know it, but it hurt my feelings.

I went to Hef and told him that Audra was a liar and out to get me, but he let her move in anyway. At one point I thought I was going to get kicked out and she was going to get my room. That really made me mad. There was a time when I wouldn't have cared, but now that everyone wanted me out and off the show, I really wanted to be there. If I was going to leave it was going to be on my own terms.

As the days went on they continued filming all of us doing our thing around the house. We were basically just being ourselves, but I could tell they were shaping us into characters. Bridget was the smart one, Holly was the nice one, and I was the athletic one. As for Audra, I don't know what she was supposed to be—the bitch? (This is my book, so I get to say that!)

I didn't mind being the athletic one and wearing jerseys so people watching the show could tell me apart from the others, but I did mind being pushed out of every scene. Audra kissed Holly's and Bridget's asses, and I could see myself quickly slipping of the picture.

The tension came to a head as the camera crews filmed us getting ready to go to Las Vegas to celebrate Carmella's birthday. Since it was her real birthday and she was one of my real friends, I went to Victoria's Secret and got her a gift card and some other little things as a present. I didn't intend for this to be on the show; I just wanted to get her a nice gift.

The night before the trip I stored the shopping bag with the present downstairs, where I could easily grab it before we headed to Las Vegas. The next day, the gift was gone. On the show they made it look like I lost it and was running around like a chicken with its head cut off looking for it. (I think the producers wanted to make me look disorganized.) But I knew it wasn't my fault. I asked everyone if they'd seen the gift. I searched the whole Mansion and thought I was losing my mind. *Where is my shit?*

Finally, I had no choice but to go to Las Vegas without the gift, and I felt terrible.

A few days later one of Audra's friends got into a fight with her over something that didn't involve me at all, and afterward she told me that Audra had stolen my bag and thrown it away. *Bitch!*

I suspected the whole time she was behind the missing bag but I never had any proof. But she'd pissed off the wrong girl, and her former friend ratted her out to everyone—Holly, Bridget, and, most important, Hef.

I was mad that I had looked like a jackass while they were filming, but at the same time I was happy because I knew it was only a matter of time before Audra's true colors would shine through. Even Holly and Bridget were mad at her, and after that incident they started to lean more toward my side. Soon after, Hef kicked Audra out and the drama was over. However, had she not gotten caught she very easily could have been the third girl on the show, and I would have been out for sure.

I was thrilled that things worked out the way they did. Audra was banned from the Mansion for a little while, and when she was allowed back, the staff and everyone at the Mansion warned her to stay away from me. I was still mad and would have beat her ass if she'd come near me.

Actually, one time I was in the gym and she walked in. We made eye contact and I totally dogged her. I gave her a look that said I was ready to fight, and she went running. (I think I picked that look up from an old boyfriend.)

None of the Audra crap was on the show because it was important to Hef that no one ever came off looking bad. He wanted the show to be about the fun times we had at the Mansion, so no drama was ever really aired.

Audra *did* make her way into one of the episodes, though. She's the one in the season one Fourth of July episode who was too fat to fit into her bunny suit. It took a team of butlers to squeeze her into a costume that gave her back cleavage. I guess what goes around comes around.

———

Speaking of bunny suits: I refused to wear one. Even before we began filming the show I always wanted to do things my way and dress the way I wanted to. I actually thought the bunny outfits were cute, but I never saw myself as a bunny, so there was no way I was getting into one of those things, especially when the cameras were around.

I did wear the suit once, before the show started filming, to *Comedy Central's Roast of Pamela Anderson*. I absolutely hated it. I put it on, and it was the most disgusting feeling in the world. Of course, when the photos from that event came out I saw that I'd had a huge camel toe, and I swore from that day on I would never wear the outfit again.

Unfortunately, Hef would get mad when I didn't wear it. He came to my room one time and had a long talk with me about it.

"Why don't you want to wear the suit?" he asked.

"It's just not me," I explained. "I'm sorry, but I just don't feel right wearing it."

We went back and forth on the subject and he was clearly frustrated. I could tell he was mad at me for feeling that way about the bunny suit, and I felt bad because I didn't want to disappoint him. But while I know it's an honor, it's not my style, and it was important for me to be me as much as possible—particularly when we were filming. I had an image I wanted to portray, and the bunny suit just didn't fit it.

When the first few episodes finally aired, I was nervous and a little embarrassed to see myself on TV. I thought it was really cool that we were getting to do the show, but I still thought it was strange to watch myself each week.

While I'd realized the producers were shaping us into characters during filming, I had no idea that by editing things a certain way they could really make us more into our characters than who we really were. I was fine being the sporty one, but it wasn't like I was always playing sports and had no other interests. Plus, I felt like I was nice enough and smart enough to have Holly and Bridget's traits every once in a while, too.

I started getting really critical of myself about things that I'd never really thought about before. If I made any sort of mistake, or even if I was kidding about something, I knew that they would edit it to make me seem ditzy. They filmed for long stretches of time, so everyone was bound to say something silly once in a while. But if I were to say the sky was green and then correct myself and say it was blue, they would edit out the correction, and I didn't like that at all. Just because Bridget was the smart one didn't mean Holly and I had to be stupid. And just because Holly was sweet didn't mean Bridget and I were crazy. All of a sudden, I wasn't so sure "sporty" was that good of a role to play.

I understood that it was better for television to make us one-dimensional, that was easier for fans of the show to relate if they could label each of us a certain way. Plus, I liked the general direction the show was going in and what it was starting to do for our lives in terms of exposure, so I wasn't about to complain.

Still, it was a lot to take in all at once. The publicists even bought us these little pairs of underwear that we had to wear. Mine said NAUGHTY. Yeah, compared to those other two I *was* naughty, but being labeled as such pissed me off. I could be nice sometimes, too.

I decided I needed to mold my character myself and do my best to make sure I came across the right way. I was into hip-hop music so I started wearing my hat to the side and playing that up, and I pumped up the sports angle more because I *was* a big sports fan. I wanted to stand out among the girls, but I wanted to stand out as me.

I was a fun girl, too, and I wanted the fans to know it. At the Fight Night party in the first season, I made sure I looked hot for all the guys but also for the cameras. Fight Night was a big party at the Mansion featuring a live boxing match and taking place the night before ESPN's ESPY Awards, so all the big athletes were there. I was ripped by then, so I was happy to show off my hard work to all the stars. That night I was drinking and shaking my ass and being an all-around crazy girl. I was excited to have a good time, and I wanted to make sure people knew that I was sporty but also fun. That seemed like a good kind of character to be.

I felt a little better once I figured out how to take some control over my character, but there were some real, non-premeditated moments as well. When Holly, Bridget, and I were told on camera that we were going to be on the cover of *Playboy*, that look of shock on my face was very real. I never thought I'd be on the cover of the magazine. I liked the way I looked at the time, with my super-fit body and my white-blonde hair, so I was excited. I called my mom and told her right away. She thought it was a real honor, and she was proud of me. It was a great opportunity.

During that first season, Bridget, Holly, and I continued to keep our distance except when we were filming. We did our own thing off camera, and there was an unspoken competition for camera time when the cameras were around. Each of us wanted the others to look good and be successful, but whether they will admit it or not, I think we each wanted the spotlight and to look the best in every episode.

At the beginning of season two, Holly and Bridget were asked to appear in a Captain Morgan ad, but you had to be twenty-five years old to appear in a liquor ad, so I was too young. I was even more disappointed than I showed in the episode. I didn't want to miss out on any of the opportunities. But then I got to do a solo spread in *Musclemag*, and it felt great to do something apart from the other girls. I didn't want to be like them. I wanted to be different, and I was up for anything that separated me from the pack.

Maybe being the sporty one wasn't that bad after all.

CHAPTER 14

Going Home a Star

As the show progressed through the second season and became more popular, we got to do cooler (and more expensive) things in each episode. We even went to Europe and took a tour of England, France, Italy, and Germany. At that point I had never been out of the country (unless you count Tijuana) and I started to realize that while plenty of Hef's past girlfriends lived great lives while in the Mansion, Holly, Bridget, and I were part of something special.

Traveling was fun, of course, but it was good for our friendship, too. For whatever reason, Holly, Bridget, and I always became closer when we took big trips—especially Bridget and me, because Holly always had Hef, and that made the two of us travel partners.

I was scared as hell of flying—I still am. I hate the whole experience. I'll grab on the sides of my seat or squeeze the arm of a complete stranger next to me during flights. I really panic, and it's terrible from start to finish. But if I'm going to fly, there is no better way to travel than on Hef's private jet. The thing is basically a mansion with wings. Bridget and I each had our own couches, and Holly and Hef always shared a bed. It was the prefect setup.

Hef's brother, Keith, and his date came with us to Europe, and everything went smoothly during the vacation. On the flight back, though, something snapped in his girlfriend's brain. Maybe the cabin pressure got to her or her seatbelt was too tight, but this girl went nuts. When we stopped in New York to go through customs and have our passports checked, out of nowhere she started going off on the airport security lady.

All this sweet, older, heavyset security woman wanted to do was check our passports, and Keith's date started yelling obscene things at her like, "Are you a lesbian? Because I'll lick your pussy!" and "Come on, baby, handcuff me!" It was one sexual taunt after another.

Holly, Bridget, and I looked at each other like, *What the hell happened to this chick?* We thought she was trying to be funny at first, but she just kept going and going. She had lost her damn mind.

Keith finally settled her down enough to get us back on the plane, but when we were taking off for Los Angeles the madness started up again. We all had to sit down and buckle up for takeoff, and she decided to sit down practically on top of Bridget. At first Bridget was fine with her sitting close by, but then the girl started leaning on her and trying to get her to move off the couch.

I started getting pissed. I told the girl to move and she started yapping and talking all kinds of shit to Bridget and me. Bridget yelled at her to get off. Then the girl began shouting, "Kendra, Kendra, Kendra," trying to get me more involved when I just wanted to survive takeoff. "Kendra, Kendra, Kendra!"

"What the fuck, bitch?" I finally yelled. "Shut the fuck up!" She's lucky I was buckled into my seat or I would have knocked her out.

"That's why I like you, Kendra," she said. "You tell it like it is." Then she started calling me a chickenhead and a bunch of other names.

I turned to Keith and said, "I'm going to knock this bitch out. Get your girl in check."

Luckily security came and grabbed her because we were seconds away from really going at it. Eventually we all settled down, but we were stuck with a crazy woman on the flight for five more hours.

Something wild *always* happened on those flights, and it seemed to bring Holly, Bridget, and me together. We became a team because even though we weren't best friends, we knew and understood one another, and we needed one another during those times.

We also stuck together when it came to fighting for what we wanted on the show.

We didn't get paid a dime to do the entire first season of *The Girls Next Door*. We had our allowance from Hef, and appearing on the show was just something we had to do as his girlfriends.

At first we didn't know where the show was going or if people were even going to watch it, so we all just went along with it. We felt like we had nothing to lose once we'd laid down the law about what we would and would not do on camera. But then the show started to take off and we knew we deserved more. We were putting in a lot of hours. Plus, we needed more clothes and makeup if we were going to be on camera all the time and constantly out at events promoting the show. No one was giving that stuff to us, so we needed to get paid to make it work.

The three of us got together and fought for a paycheck. We went to Hef and told him that we deserved to be paid, and he made sure the producers of the show knew we needed some sort of payment to continue.

Eventually we won. It was a minor victory, though, because it's not like were were getting tons of cash for doing the second season. But it was a good start, and it showed that even if our personalities were very different, Holly, Bridget, and I could come together when we needed to.

The show tried to hype up some sort of jealousy among us and imply that Holly was protective of Hef and didn't like when Bridget or I got any attention, but I think that was more television than reality. About two and a half years after I moved in, our nights with Hef came to an end. I don't know if it was Holly's influence or if Hef lost interest or what, but one night after a party he went upstairs without us. I looked around for some sort of signal that it was time to party, but I saw nothing. And just like that, it was over. I thought, *Cool.*

From that point on, Holly had Hef all to herself. If there was any weird tension before, it was gone now. The end of those evenings probably helped us become stronger as a group. You'd be surprised at how not getting naked and sleeping with a guy at the same time can do wonders for a friendship.

My popularity on the show and the success of the show overall also helped me fit in a little better. When the girls saw that I was an asset to the show they realized that maybe I was someone worth getting to know. The fans appreciated me, and Holly and Bridget respected that. It was important for me to have their respect because it allowed us to have good working relationship. And at the end of the day, we all accepted one another for who we were, and it felt good to be one of the girls.

Just as I was starting to feel like an equal, the producers of the show decided they wanted to take everyone to my hometown to film an episode. I was always afraid of my two worlds colliding, because I didn't want any of the people I used to hang out with to resurface and get involved in my new life. I also knew that even though I was proud of where I came from, my neighborhood wasn't exactly what the girls had in mind for a weekend getaway, and I hated the idea of being judged by them.

But it was exciting, too. I heard Hef had never been to a girlfriend's house before, so I was honored that he chose me to be the first. Obviously, I lived the closest, but I knew he also genuinely cared about me. We shared more of a friendship than a romantic relationship, but I knew I was special to Hef. We had a bond.

All the highlights from that experience were on the episode—including every neighbor peeking their heads out of their windows to watch us film. They were all such gossips.

That's why it pissed me off when Holly said in the episode that I called my hometown a ghetto. I *never* said that. Maybe I acted ghetto, but I'm not from the ghetto, and I would never say that about my neighborhood. When it aired, everyone back home was mad at me. It was the only time I got really pissed off at the show. I feel like I'm still explaining myself to people back home about that.

Whether we filmed in San Diego or not, it was only a matter of time—with or without the show—before someone from my past who I didn't want to see found me again.

Not surprisingly, it was Zack, still only a couple of years removed from being husband material, who decided to reach out first. I started getting phone calls and e-mails from him saying that he missed me and loved me and wanted me to come home. I know I told him that I would stay at the Mansion only a couple of months, but I thought he understood that was really a good-bye.

Whenever he called I would apologize and say, "This is my life now. It has to be this way." It was tough. But then it got scary.

Zack was pissed, and I guess he wanted to get back at me for leaving him. He started posting naked photos of me from when I was seventeen on my MySpace page. Somehow he'd gotten into my page and decided to do some damage. When I found out, I thought, *Hell, no—this is not happening.* I flipped out. Crying, I ran to Hef and told him what was going on. He said he'd take care of it, and it all went away.

Other than a few experiences like that early on, I knew that as the show grew, life in the Mansion would only get better for me. I also knew that it wasn't going to last forever and if I wanted to make the most of my current situation, I had to act quickly.

Even when I was working at Papa John's I was good at saving my money, but I wanted to do more than just save my paychecks from the show, and I was worried the opportunities weren't going to be there when the show finished.

I started to get nervous that I wasn't doing enough to prepare myself for the future. Holly had Hef and she thought she would live with him in the Mansion forever. Bridget had a master's degree. What did I have to fall back on? Massage therapy school, flipping pizzas, and scraping plaque off teeth were my only areas of professional expertise, unless you count stripping. And I could never go back to stripping.

I decided to talk to Hef about my problems.

"What happens when the show ends and I get kicked out of here, Hef?" I asked. "I'll be living on the streets."

He laughed. "You'll never be on the streets, darling," he reassured me. "As long as I'm here you will be just fine."

I had a great connection with Hef; it wasn't the same kind of relationship that Holly had with him, but he was always there for me and he could always make me feel better about anything. He had promised I would never be on the streets, and I believed him. But I also knew that I had to take matters into my own hands to guarantee it.

Even before the show started I had wanted to get into acting. I found jobs as an extra posted on Craigslist and went for them on my own, without an agent or anyone helping me. I even booked a job on the show *Las Vegas*, all on my own. It was great.

I met Jon Lovitz and James Caan, and I even talked to James about Hef and the Mansion. He told me he'd lived in my room for a couple of months. It was crazy. Then I was supposed to be an extra in a movie with the actor Kevin James, and the day of the shoot I waited for fifteen hours to do my part. I kept asking when it was my turn. It was freezing out and I was starting to get sick. Finally the day ended and they told me they weren't going to need me. *What the fuck?* I was so pissed. That was the end of being an extra for me.

Once I was on *The Girls Next Door*, I knew I could book bigger roles, but I had to go about things differently. Craigslist wasn't going to cut it. I needed an agent and a manager and other professionals to book me paying gigs.

A producer I met on *Las Vegas* kept in touch, and with the right amount of ass-kissing I was able to get back on the show, this time with a one-line speaking part. I was in a scene with Josh Duhamel and James Caan, and I played a waitress who had to say "Do you want a drink?" or something like that. I practiced over and over, and when the day was done I officially had the acting bug.

Shortly after that I met Robert Miano, an actor who was in one of my favorite movies, *Donnie Brasco*. He was also an acting coach so I decided to use some of the money I was making from *The Girls Next Door* to take acting lessons. It seemed like a good investment and I thought down the road it could really pay off. No one even knew I was taking the classes. I just did it on my own, and I loved it. It was my plan for the future.

Shortly after my *Las Vegas* gig, I went down to San Diego for a weekend. Hef would let me go there to visit my mom from time to time, and usually I broke the rules while I was there and spent the nights partying with guys. One night I was out and talking to some friends about how I wanted to do more with whatever fame I was getting from the show, and one guy mentioned that he had an agent friend he would introduce me to.

The agent and I spoke on the phone and I was so excited— it seemed like the acting thing was really going to happen for me. Hef wanted me to be happy, and he was cool with me doing whatever I wanted to do to pursue my dreams, but when his team at *Playboy* read the contract the agent sent me, they warned me that signing with him was a bad idea. It turned out the guy was a sports agent, not an entertainment agent, and things didn't seem right. I didn't care. I just wanted to make money, so I signed the contract.

My new agent didn't book me acting gigs; instead, he booked me for appearances at nightclubs and other venues around the country. That was fine with me. As long as I was making money, I didn't care.

My first appearance was in Cincinnati, Ohio. Hef sent Joe, the *Playboy* security guard, with me for two reasons: to keep me safe, and to make sure I didn't hook up with any guys. I could leave during the day and go shopping or to classes by myself. I could even visit my mom by myself. But if I was going to be out at night and I wasn't staying with my mom, Hef always made sure Joe was with me.

I got a small amount for that first appearance, and my agent took a 20-percent cut. Still, money was money and I was happy. More offers started to come in after that, and I pointed out that rather than doing a million appearances for small fees, maybe I could do fewer and charge more money (as an agent he should have figured that out). It worked out, and before I knew it I was making good money.

Even though I knew my agent wasn't the best, he became a friend and I was loyal so I stuck with him. The appearances allowed me to send money to my mom and pay her back, in a way, for putting up with me through all the hard times, and every other penny went right in the bank so I could put my fear of living on the streets to rest.

It felt good to be controlling my own destiny. It was also nice get out and be in the spotlight a little without the other girls. I enjoyed that. Everything was going really well, until my skin started to break out. Then I just wanted the spotlight to go away.

CHAPTER 15

Breakout Star

*T*he success of the show was really exciting for all of us, but with fame came a new batch of worries.

Throughout my life, the way I saw myself always changed based on what was going on around me. If I didn't fit in at school or if I had a teacher tell me I wasn't smart, I got down on myself. But when I landed a new job or was in a position that made me feel pretty, my confidence shot back up.

Filming *The Girls Next Door* created a roller coaster of emotions, and by the time the show was in its third season, I was due for a free fall.

Holly, Bridget, and I were popular enough at that point to have a big fan base, and also our share of haters. Maybe it was my inexperience with celebrity, but I took everything that was said about me to heart, and Google became my worst enemy.

I'd go on the Internet and type in my name, and all these blogs, fan sites, and random news stories would pop up. Most of them were flattering, but my eyes always seemed to wander toward the negative ones. Trust me, there was some evil shit on there. People would call me dumb and I'd log on and type "Fuck you" in the comment box.

These people had something to say about everything. Even when I did something so minor as refuse to wear the bunny suit in an episode when we were meeting the troops, fans gave me a really hard time. I wanted to greet the soldiers as me, Kendra Wilkinson, not as some girl dressed like a rabbit. My grandfather taught me to respect our troops, and it seemed more respectful to meet them in normal-looking clothes. But people all over the Internet disagreed. They knew I was anti-bunny and saw it as a slap in the face to Hef and the *Playboy* brand.

I knew in my heart that I was right to stand up for myself, but it started to seem like I just couldn't win. No matter what I did, someone on some Web site had something to say about it. I became really critical of myself and started to dislike how I was being portrayed in the public eye. I blamed myself and was really unhappy.

Then, in the winter of 2006, I rolled out of bed, caught my reflection in the mirror, and saw that my face had broken out with a terrible case of acne. It started around Thanksgiving, and by Christmas my face was covered in angry red spots. The Christmas episode, "Snow Place Like Home," didn't air until March of the following year, but I knew when they were filming that as soon as it ran I would be seeing comments all over the Internet about it. I was really depressed that whole season about the acne, but filming Christmas night was the worst.

I never had acne as a kid, so I didn't have an it-happens-to-everyone attitude. I wasn't even sure where it came from. Maybe it was stress. Maybe it was all the holiday chocolate I was eating. Either way, my face was covered with pimples, and I wanted to stay as far away from the cameras as possible.

Unfortunately, I didn't really have a choice. The production crew had put snow all over the front lawn and was getting ready to film a fun holiday party. I was a real bitch about being on camera and complained like crazy, but none of it mattered. The producers weren't going to let me hide. The show didn't have a makeup team, so the acne wasn't going to hide, either. I was mortified.

I started to break down. I couldn't go to the Christmas party; I didn't even want to leave my room! I locked the door and refused to come out.

The producers were not happy. They started yelling for me to get out of the room, but I just wanted to crawl under my covers and hide. Eventually Hef came up to my room, and when he walked in I started crying.

"Look how bad it is," I said.

"They're just love bites," he said before kissing my forehead. "You're still so beautiful."

I wiped my tears away and smiled. He always said the right thing. When I gained a little weight during my first year at the Mansion he gave me the tough love, but this time he knew it was a different situation. He knew I was down on myself and stressed out. And after just a few kind words from Hef I was feeling better.

I went down to the party. I hid from the cameras at first, but then I loosened up a bit and stopped caring, and I even ended up having a pretty good time. But after that night I continued to stay out of as many shots as possible. Hef saw how concerned I was about the acne so he paid to put me on Accutane. They say that stuff messes with your head and makes you suicidal, but I was as down as I could possibly be before taking it, so mentally there was nowhere to go but up.

Physically, though, my face got worse when I started the medication. That's what is supposed to happen, but I still wasn't happy about it when it did. I had big red blotches everywhere and I was near tears every time the camera was on me. By that point I knew what the producers wanted so I gave it to them as quickly as possible and then got out of there as fast as I could.

When the episodes started to air, people commented on the Internet about my acne, just as I'd feared. They called me ugly, and it just killed me because there was nothing I could do about it.

After about eight months of my taking Accutane, scrubbing my face twenty times a day, and picking at every stupid blemish on my skin, the acne finally went away.

As if getting called ugly on the Internet wasn't bad enough, as I watched the episodes, I got pissed because I wasn't in any of them. I complained to the producers that the episodes were all Bridget or all Holly, and they reminded me that I chose to not be in them. We fought back and forth, and in the end the only person I could really blame was myself. I needed the confidence to not care what anybody was saying about me. I didn't look in the mirror and see my good qualities, instead, I focused on the acne. (I also blamed chocolate. I haven't eaten chocolate since that winter; in fact, I've almost developed a fear of it.)

By season four things were looking up. We got a raise each year, so I was finally making enough from the show to be able to actually do a few things with my money.

I did some research online and talked to a few friends, and eventually I decided to invest the money in real estate. I found a condo in La Jolla that I bought and fixed up myself, with the help of my grandfather. He started to get pretty sick right after we finished, and I felt really lucky that he was able to stay alive long enough to see great things happen for me.

Soon after fixing up the condo, I bought a second house. I let my mom manage both of the properties and take care of the renters. It was such a rush to be doing something for my future, and making smart decisions with my money.

The show remained really popular, and it was cool to feel like a star. I loved hearing that fans thought I was funny or watched the show for me specifically. Who doesn't love feeling special? But the show and the celebrity that comes with it wasn't what got me going. It was power. Buying those houses made me feel powerful. Fame was cool, but power was better.

I always wondered what the people from my past might think if they saw me succeed at something. And while it was great knowing that they were watching me play a character named Kendra on the show, I was more curious about what they would think if they saw me buying houses and making a business for myself beyond television. By season four I could finally walk around with my head held high and say, *Look at me now, mother-fuckers!*

It was a great year. During filming I got to show off my racing skills from back in the day at the Long Beach Grand Prix (and kick George Lucas's butt on the track while doing it). I think that was probably the coolest thing I got to do while living in the Mansion.

We also went to Alaska to see where Holly grew up and nearly died on a floatplane while there, which was not so cool. The engine on the plane almost blew out, and when I smelled the smoke and heard the noises I freaked out. I don't know why they kept putting me on planes when they knew I hated to fly, but that incident was especially terrifying. I nearly drank myself to death that day because I was so scared.

I also met Brittany Binger, a 2007 Playmate, that year, and we became close friends. She's a quiet, conservative girl from Ohio—the complete opposite of me—but somehow we got along really well. I taught her things about life at the Mansion, gave her sex advice, and did my best to bring out her fun, naughty side; it felt good to be in a position at *Playboy* where I felt confident enough to pass on some of my wisdom. Brittany was there for me, too, and she's still one of my closest friends. She's always helping me to be a better person and to think before I act.

I loved that I was doing well and in a position to help others. That year I paid for a face-lift for my mom, and for her to get her boobs done before *Playboy*'s annual Midsummer Night's Dream Party. After my dad left, my mom never really put herself out there to meet anyone. She gave up on men, and on some level, she gave up on herself. It felt good to be able to help boost her confidence a little, and I think she became a whole new woman after those procedures. She feels young again—and she acts like it, too. She began to love going to *Playboy* parties, and she even joined Facebook and Twitter. She also started filling me in on other reality shows on TV, and on all the gossip she reads online. She even goes into chat rooms and talks shit to teenagers! It's pretty funny, and I'm glad I could help her live a little.

Having money gave me a new sense of freedom and comfort in life. I felt like I was in control of things for a change.

Life wasn't completely drama-free, though.

Around that time, I was supposed to be in Eminem's "Smack That" video, and when I found out I was really excited. I was a good dancer so I thought it would be a fun way to show off my dancing skills. Plus, my friend Brittany from San Diego was a huge Eminem fan, so she drove two hours to come with me. The night before we were so pumped that we couldn't sleep. We drove downtown at six A.M. I got my hair done, and then I sat and waited for eleven hours.

During the day, Eminem was nice to us. "You're from *Playboy*, right?" he said. I was so stoked that he even knew my name.

Then, a little later, things changed. During another break I was sitting across from him and he yelled out something about San Diego. I didn't know what the hell he was talking about but I wondered if he was on something. He got up and came over to where I was sitting and out of nowhere started yelling like a complete psycho and pouring water all over me. I was pissed.

I got up and punched him in his side and yelled right back. "You're a little bitch," I shouted. "You're always picking on girls. You're not a man."

I went off, and then I went on MySpace and wrote an angry message about him. I didn't think about the show or the fans or anything. I just blurted out all my feeling about him. That was a mistake. I was acting like my mom would on the Internet, but really I needed Brittany Binger to remind me to think before I acted. Where the hell was she?

Then the drama turned to the business world. The agent I had at the time—the one who made those rookie mistakes when booking my appearances—tried to expand my "brand" to include clothing and failed miserably.

He attempted to negotiate a clothing-line deal for me with some guys from Dubai, and it was supposedly going to pay me millions. He kept saying how great this opportunity was, so I signed the contracts. The plan was to put out a line of shirts called K-Dub, and I even hosted a launch party at Pure Night-club in Las Vegas, where I threw out shirts to the crowd like a jackass. But it turned out that the Dubai guys were complete con artists. The whole deal was fake.

With the help of some lawyers I put an end to it—and severed my relationship with my agent, too. I knew it was time for me to make bigger moves, and I couldn't do that with him.

Among my more fun ventures that year was when I did a reality show called *Celebrity Rap Superstar*, where I competed against other stars in a rap competition. It was a blast. I was surrounded by all these rappers I grew up listening to. I think hip-hop music was so much better back then, so I was honored to be working alongside guys like Warren G. and Redman.

When the producers called and asked me if I wanted to be on the show, I insisted that they put me with Too Short. In my opinion, he was the best. Too Short taught me how to rap, but he also mentored me about being a celebrity and how important it was for me to treat my fans well.

Even though Too Short was a good teacher, I knew I wasn't really a rapper, so I figured I would give the people what they wanted. Each week I just went up there and shook my ass for the crowd. My ass-shaking got me all the way to the finals.

The final week, we had to come up with a rap about our lives, and in a few verses let the world know where we came from. It was quite a task since my life was filled with some crazy stories, but with Too Short's help I put it all together. It went:

Little girl be you, 'cause I got to be me.
Live your own life, be all you can be.
And if the sky turns gray,
It's okay.
Just keep working hard, and you'll shine one day.
This is a story about a Playmate,
You might think my life was always great.
You see me on TV when my booty shake.
But now it's time to get the story straight.

When I was young, my dad was ghost.
Left me and mom on the West Coast.
Just little K-Dub growing up in Diego.
People doing drugs and I couldn't say no.
I hit rock bottom. I hit so low.
People tried to help me, I said hell no.

I didn't win, but I was proud as hell to rap my story, so it didn't matter. And I didn't have to shake my ass to get the crowd to feel me. I went out there and said "Enough of this stupid shit; listen to my real story," and people were blown away. The judges loved it; Hef, who was there supporting me, loved it; and everyone in the audience respected me for what I'd done. I'd never felt so good in my life.

CHAPTER 16

When Kendra Met Hank

By the beginning of 2008 I was getting antsy. Living at the Playboy Mansion with Hef and the girls and filming the same show for four straight years was the biggest commitment I'd ever made.

I like change, and I need change, so I knew I was due for a big move.

The thing is, I usually just let nature take its course and guide me. I could have left Zack at any time, but it wasn't until Hef called that I took action. This time around, I knew it was only a matter of time before the show came to an end, and while I was prepared financially I wasn't sure what I was going to do with my life. But I was ready for a big move, and I knew that sooner or later something (or someone) would help me kick off the next phase.

The problem, of course, was that it was nearly impossible to meet anyone who could sweep me off my feet while I was living at the Mansion. When we weren't out with Hef, we still had a nine P.M. curfew—even after the show became a hit. And if we were out late promoting the show or doing appearances, we always had a bodyguard with us, watching our every move.

The Mansion was locked up tighter than Fort Knox. Even as a kid, I was always sneaking out, and if I got caught I could run away. But the Mansion was different. With a hit TV show and a man I respected too much to disappoint, there was no getting caught or running away.

But a girl's got needs!

I'd have a fun fling with a guy every now and then, but it was nearly impossible to have a real relationship when I was always looking over my shoulder. It was getting pretty frustrating. And then, on March 27, 2008, at the Playboy Golf Classic in the City of Industry, California, I met Hank Baskett.

Hank thinks he tells the story of how we met better, but since this is my book I get to do the talking. That said, in the spirit of compromise (which is an important part of marriage), I've included parts of his side of the story here as well.

So, I was at the Classic, looking really cute in my tiny gold skirt, when the event coordinator came up to me and asked me if I knew Hank Baskett. She'd told me a little about him ahead of time, but I hadn't really thought much of it. Hank says that before that, the same coordinator had called him and asked if he wanted to meet me. Hank knew I liked sports, and from what he had seen it seemed like I was a wonderful person (his words, not mine), so he thought it would be cool to meet me. So the day of the golf tournament he knew we were going to meet, but he didn't want me to know that he knew who I was. Smooth move.

In addition to what the event coordinator told me, I watched the Eagles and remembered seeing him score a touchdown against the Cowboys. I thought he was a tight end (he wasn't, but in any case I thought he was a pretty awesome player). The event coordinator told me he had a crush on me (Hank, of course, denies this) and wanted to meet me. I thought he was kind of my style, but I'd never really had someone try to hook me up with a guy like that before, so I was a bit hesitant.

The morning of the tournament Hank was on the driving range talking with my friend Shaun Phillips from the San Diego Chargers when he spotted me posing for photos. Shaun walked over and started talking to me, and then brought me over to meet Hank. He introduced himself in this deep voice—"Hi, I'm Hank Baskett"—that I just loved. A photographer at the event took a photo of us right at that moment, so we have a photo from the first second we met. In it, we look like we're already together. We look married in that picture, like we are meant to be a couple—it's so weird.

I asked Hank which course he was playing, and when I realized we were on different courses I got upset. But Hank wasn't going to try to switch and cause trouble, so we had no choice but to go our separate ways. I found out later that right when we walked away from each other Hank called his best friend and told him all about me.

I spent the whole day on my assigned course, drinking and having fun with other athletes. Shaun was on my course, and I bugged him all day about Hank. I told him that I thought Hank was cute, and I wanted him to pass the message along, since I wasn't sure if I gave off the right signals during our first meeting. I had acted shy, which I never do.

Toward the end of the day, Joe, my *Playboy* security guard, came over to me and told me I had to leave for Las Vegas. We were going there to film the episode in which Stacy Burke, one of Hef's former girlfriends, got married, and I had to be there. I had never been so upset about having to go to Vegas in my life. I argued with Joe for an hour, but I didn't have a choice. I had to go. So I hopped in Joe's golf cart and we started driving toward the clubhouse. Hank just happened to be finishing his first nine holes and was passing the clubhouse right as I was driving by with Joe.

If I had left right away, I would have missed Hank altogether. But he saw me, and he saw me see him. I screamed "Hey!" and made Joe stop the golf cart. Hank started coming toward me and I liked the way he walked. He looked cool, but not like some cocky asshole. I could tell just by the way he walked that he was confident but also a good guy, so I asked for his number.

We joke about this now because you would think that Hank would have asked me for my number first, but Hank says he thought I was so nice and so real, he just clammed up. So I got his number and told him I had to leave for Vegas, and he thought he would never hear from me again. Later that day I texted him: "Hey, it's Kendra, what's up?"

He couldn't believe I had texted. Apparently he had been hearing my laugh in his head all day (or so he says), so he was really happy—and shocked—to get my message. We texted back and forth about seeing each other at the post-Classic party the next night.

I rushed back from Vegas so I could make it to the party. We were shooting the show that day and the filming was taking forever so I was nervous I wasn't going to make it. I got to L.A. at eleven P.M. and the party was over at one A.M., so as soon as I got there I ran in and started looking all over for him.

When we finally found each other we were really excited. I went up to Hank and gave him a hug. My friends—like Shaun, and Vernon Davis of the San Francisco 49ers—were on the other side of the room, so I told him I had to go over there and be with them. I guess he was a little shocked—he thought we were going to hang out, and although I was thinking about him the whole time, it's not like I could ditch my friends. Plus, I was a crazy party girl back then and I always just bounced around the room and got drunk. I wasn't trying to mess with him. I liked him, and my friends could see it. But I had to be careful about who I was seen spending time with, and even though he was disappointed that was just how it had to be.

I texted him first thing the next morning as he was getting on a plane. When he got home that night, we spoke on the phone and it went really well. He was so easy to talk to and we had so many things in common, and between sports, music, and our families, there was so much to talk about. I didn't know if things were going to get romantic between us, but I was open to seeing how things went. I decided I was just going to wait and see with Hank.

We've talked every day since that first phone call. Our conversations would last for hours, and what started off as a friendship grew into a relationship unlike anything I have ever had. It was just . . . perfect.

———

It was pretty crazy how Hank and I hit it off right away. We talked as often as possible. I would just sit in my room at the Mansion, away from everyone else, and talk to him. No topic was off-limits. I would tell him the most off-the-wall things about myself, and while sometimes I think he thought I was crazy, he didn't run away, which was a good sign.

We had plenty of real conversations, too. In a sad coincidence, early in our relationship both my grandfather and his grandmother died, in the same week. Hank called me to tell me she had passed away while I was in the hospital with my grandfather. I sat on the phone with him while I held my grandfather's hand, and we opened up to each other and bonded a lot during that difficult time. I knew by the way he talked about his grandmother that he was someone special, and I know Hank would say the same thing about me and my grandfather.

I could have talked to any of my closest friends about my feelings when my grandfather was dying, and he could have called any of his friends. But we chose each other, even after just hanging out for one day. I found comfort in his voice. We grew closer not so much romantically but spiritually, and for the first time in my life, that actually seemed like the better option.

I got to know his heart and his intentions. I knew that he was in this because he was a caring person, and that there was a special bond between us. I also knew that we could be more than friends.

Toward the beginning of the summer I was invited down to San Diego to throw out the first pitch at a Padres game. That was a huge honor for me. I grew up going to games with my grandfather, and I was a big Padres fan.

I called Hank and told him what a big deal it was for me. My mom, my grandmother, my brother, and my childhood friend Brittany—all the people who were important in my life—were going to be there, and I wanted Hank to be a part of that group. It took a little courage on my part, but I told him it would mean the world to me if he came.

Although I spent every free second in my room talking to Hank, this was a big step. Talking was one thing; having him come to San Diego was another. But I was ready. He was ready, too, and he agreed to come.

We decided that I would pick him up at LAX and we'd drive down to San Diego together. As I left the Mansion, I was nervous. I didn't know how it would feel to be with Hank in person. So much had changed since we first met. We were a lot closer, but I thought it might be awkward to be with him in the flesh.

I'd been worrying about being face-to-face with him for days, but since I was still living at the Mansion and I was still Hef's girlfriend I couldn't talk to anyone about it. I had to deal with the emotions on my own.

I also had to be very careful to make sure we didn't get caught. I wasn't sure where this relationship was going yet and

I didn't want to ruin the show or be disrespectful to Hef, especially after all he'd done for me. But at the same time, everyone at the Mansion could tell that I was drifting away from my life there, even Hef. He knew something was up. Before I met Hank, I was always excited to get out and party, and now I was constantly holed up in my room. Everyone could tell I was different. Still, I tried to be slick.

I left the Mansion in pink pajama pants, a gray and white sweatshirt, and a pair of earrings. I'm not a jewelry person; I hate having anything dangling on me, and I never wore jewelry at the Playboy Mansion, so when I walked out in earrings, all the butlers knew something was up. I looked too cute for a drive to my mother's house. Carlena asked me about it and I didn't lie—I told her I was going to the airport first. I just didn't tell her who I was picking up. Since I was going to San Diego to my mom's house I didn't have a bodyguard with me, so I really didn't have to answer to anyone.

I was feeling shy and nervous when I got to the airport. Hank's flight was delayed about forty-five minutes, which was fine because I was thirty minutes late anyway. I parked the car and waited for him, trying to stay incognito. My cell phone didn't work in the parking garage outside the US Airways terminal, so I hid behind a bush just outside the garage and waited. It was pretty sneaky.

He finally came outside and we shared a long hug and a quick kiss on the cheek. We were both way too tense for some big makeout session. Plus, he was very respectful, so that wouldn't have been his style.

As we were pulling out of the garage I realized that I had lost my parking ticket. I got really mad at myself because I didn't want him to think I was unorganized or some sort of idiot, but he didn't judge me.

Finally we got out of LAX and began the two-hour drive to San Diego. We started off with nervous talk—I think I asked him how the flight was about fifty times—but then, about thirty minutes in, I just thought *Screw it*—it was time to get real. I felt like now was as good a time as any to tell him my whole life story, so I did.

I told him everything. I talked about my dad, the drugs, the psych ward, running away from home, cutting, stripping—*everything*! I even told him that I wanted to be a mom and have a family someday. He needed to know the real me, and I thought the best way to make that happen was to just put it all out there. I thought he was going to open the car door and jump out a few times, but he didn't. Instead, he told me about his childhood and his family and the charity work he does.

All of my past relationships had started off with sex. I would jump right into a physical relationship without knowing the guy at all. This was different. Between the hours on the phone and the two-hour car ride, Hank and I knew each other as well, if not better, than anyone else—and we hadn't even kissed yet.

When we got to our hotel in San Diego we were so tired we passed out face-to-face on the bed. The next day I had to do a radio show at seven A.M. Hank came with me, and I told the nosey radio DJs that he was a family friend. They bought it.

Afterward I took Hank to my mom's house and introduced him to my family. He found all the baby books my mom had made about me and flipped through them. I was so embarrassed.

Then he got a lecture from my grandmother about what kind of girl I was (a very special one) and what he needed to do for me (treat me very well). It was funny because our relationship was so new, but considering the circumstances it seemed serious all of a sudden.

That night I threw out the first pitch, wearing my Padres jersey (Hank didn't have a jersey, so I made him go with my brother to buy one before the game). It was so exciting. The fans were cheering, and everyone I cared about was there.

After I'd done my duty I joined my friends and family in a box to watch the game. Hank and I couldn't let anyone think that we were together so we tried to keep our distance in the box. My family knew, and Brittany could tell something was up, but it was a big secret we had to keep from everyone else.

After the game Hank and I went back to the hotel. Hank had called ahead and had them run a bath so it was all ready when we got there. We both knew this was the big night, and we both had a lot running through our heads.

When we got to our room, Hank went into the bathroom and got in the tub. I stayed outside for a second—I didn't know if he wanted me to watch him get in or if he wanted some privacy. Then I walked into the bathroom wearing only my Padres jersey. That's every guy's fantasy, isn't it? But he wasn't looking! I thought, *Okay, there's respectful, and then there is just crazy.*

"Look at me, Hank," I said.

He turned around and I slowly unbuttoned the jersey.

"You look so beautiful," he said.

I got in the tub with him, and Hank Baskett officially became my boyfriend.

CHAPTER 17

No Flash-in-the-Pan Relationship

After that amazing night in San Diego, we woke up as one happy couple. We had breakfast in our hotel room, which overlooked the bay. It was very romantic, and as I looked at Hank I knew we had something special. We shared a connection that was just so perfect—almost *too* perfect. It kind of freaked me out.

Things were going well, but my guard was definitely up. What if he went back to Philadelphia and forgot all about me? I had never been in a long-distance relationship before, and I was very nervous and afraid of getting hurt. But our relationship was built on hours and hours of conversation, so the one thing I wasn't afraid of was telling Hank how I felt.

"What's going to happen to us?" I asked over breakfast.

"What do you want to happen?" he replied.

Don't you hate when a guy answers a question with another question?

"You never know unless you try," he said eventually.

I wanted to try. The truth was, we both had the same fears, but we both knew we wanted to do whatever it took to give a relationship our best shot. No matter how it worked out down the road, I knew I wasn't ready for our time together to end. We needed at least one more night, so I came up with a plan.

After breakfast we went to my mom's house. While I was there I called the Mansion and told them I was spending another night at my mom's. Then I told my mom that if anyone from the Mansion called she should say I was in the shower and that I would call them back. She should then call me immediately, and I would call the Mansion back from my cell phone. My mom—although not exactly the best liar in the world—was up for it. She knew this was important to me.

Hank and I said our good-byes to my family, and then we drove up to L.A., where we booked a hotel room for the night. By that point I wasn't worried about getting caught at all. I knew the drill. Someone from the Mansion would call looking for me, but no one would question my mom. The toughest part would be going back to the Mansion the next day. Someone there would ask me about my trip and I would have to keep the same story going.

I wasn't sure how Hank felt about all the lying. He was probably looking for a normal relationship, but I just couldn't give that to him at the moment. I had to think about the show and Hef. I needed to honor my responsibilities. I couldn't just bail on everything just yet. On the ride back to L.A. we talked about the situation a little. This was clearly the beginning of something great, so some sacrifices would have to be made.

As it turned out, Hank knew a lot about keeping relationships secret. Hank's dad is black and his mom is white and she grew up in Louisiana, in a part of the Deep South that didn't accept interracial relationships at the time they started dating.

His mom kept her relationship with his dad a secret from her family. When she got pregnant and her family asked if she was keeping the baby, she told them that after she gave birth the baby would live with his father, and that their relationship was over. She'd go home to visit her parents and basically pretend that Hank didn't exist.

When Hank was in college, his mom's parents passed away, and his mom didn't want to keep the secret anymore. So she moved forward with her life openly and honestly. The whole time, Hank understood. He says he doesn't blame anyone, and considers his mother's need for secrecy a sign of the times. Whenever the topic of racism comes up he always says that you really have to experience it firsthand to understand what it's like.

Compared to the secrets he grew up with, what I was asking him to do seemed silly. I promised that the sneakiness wouldn't last long, and he was okay with it.

As if that wasn't enough, on the ride back to L.A., I decided to really put Hank to the test: I put on some country music.

"You may not like this," I said as I popped in a Kenny Chesney CD.

"I love country music," he said.

I couldn't believe it. I thought, *This guy is perfect*. We listened to Kenny the whole ride back to L.A., and when we got to our hotel we took all my country CDs up to the room.

The first song Hank played was "I Cross My Heart" by George Strait. When the music started, he took my hands and began spinning me around. I had always been a good dancer, but more in a hip-hop, booty-shaking kind of way. This kind of dancing was very different, and I had no idea what I was doing.

Hank taught me a two-step dance. It was so much fun! Even better, the whole time we were dancing we didn't worry about anyone or anything else. I wasn't Hugh Hefner's girlfriend who lived at the Playboy Mansion, and he wasn't a football player returning to Philadelphia in a few hours. We were two kids dancing around a hotel room without a care in the world.

I never thought I would find someone like him. I always did whatever I wanted in front of people and didn't care. I walked through school in a bikini! And here was this guy dipping me and dancing around like a cowboy, with no fear of what was going through my head. He was so comfortable in his own skin, and grew more confident with each dance step. I loved that about him.

We stayed up until five A.M., and a few hours later I dropped him off at the airport, kissed him good-bye, and returned to being the Kendra Wilkinson the rest of the world knew. Saying good-bye was not easy for me. After the amazing weekend together it was hard to not have him close by.

Laurie, a chef who started cooking at the Mansion about three years after I moved in, became a good friend, and knew me well enough that if I tried to keep a secret from her she would figure it out. From all the times I opened up to her while she taught me how to cook soul food, she'd learned to take one look at me and know something was up. So when I got back I had to tell her about Hank. She was really happy for me; she knew that I was excited about my relationship, and she told me to focus on all the positive things about it instead of the fact that he was so far away. That helped, but coping with the distance was still hard.

Luckily I was also able to keep busy, so I had a lot of distractions. That year, I had so many appearances and promotional gigs it was almost a full-time job. At least two days a week I would fly somewhere for an event, and the rest of the time I was busy with the show.

A couple of months later, Hank and I were ready for our next date. The plan was to go back to San Diego for the Del Mar Fair, which is a big county fair with rides, games, and awesome food. I went every year as a kid. I wasn't too concerned about my cover story. It was getting easier and easier to leave the Mansion at that point; I think everyone knew my days there were nearing an end.

I was so excited to see Hank again, and making the trip all the more special was the fact that he was bringing his parents to meet me. Hank and I were both nervous—meeting the parents is a big deal. He didn't really tell his mom much about me ahead of time, and he warned me that she could be rough on girls he brought around, so I didn't really know what to expect.

Before heading down to San Diego, we all met at Houston's for dinner in L.A. We started with small talk, and his mom and I realized that we both like our hamburgers well done and that neither of us likes seafood. Then Hank's dad and I bonded when he found out that I like golf. Once I told him that, I was totally in.

Then Hank and I explained a little about *Playboy* and what I did there. His parents didn't really ask questions, but I felt the need to be open with them about my life. His mom was concerned about what people would say and think about Hank and me if it got out that we were dating, since I did live at the Mansion. She wasn't judging me—she was just as concerned for me as she was for Hank—and I felt like she was on my side, too.

"People just see you for twenty minutes on TV each week and they think they know you," she said. "But that's not you."

It turned out that she was right. Hank's hometown of Clovis, New Mexico, had a big billboard up of Hank that said HOMETOWN HERO; they later took it down, when they found out he was dating me. It's a religious town and they didn't like my connection to *Playboy*, and that pissed me off. I went on some city Web site and wrote that I was going to buy every billboard in town and put our picture on it. (I still might do that, someday!)

Hank's mom wasn't like some of the other people in that town, who jumped at the chance to judge me. She understood me. I was Hugh Hefner's girlfriend, but that was just part of who I was, just like being a football player was only part of what defined Hank. Both of us were more than that. I love my family and my dogs and I'm a normal person, and both of Hank's parents realized that right away.

Any anxiety I felt before meeting them quickly went away. I even had Hank's mom laughing at one point. Hank was stunned—he couldn't believe how well we were getting along. The next day when we went to the fair his mom and I were talking like best friends. By the end of the weekend his mom had nicknamed me "Little Bit" and we were practically family already. I reassured his parents that I would never do anything to hurt Hank and that we both were going to do our best to make our relationship last, and as I was saying good-bye I asked them to remember the girl they met and to not believe everything they read on the Internet.

It was a great weekend, but afterward I was back at the Mansion and Hank was back in Philly. Being apart was hard for both of us, and the closer we got, the more difficult it became for Hank to handle my job at *Playboy*.

I was still going to club appearances and parties looking sexy—it was my job. A club was like my office, and the crowd was my boss. I had to give them what they wanted. Bits and pieces of those nights would end up on the Internet, and it became tough for Hank to deal with my public persona when he could only see me in private.

Our relationship was still secret, so it's not like he could talk to a friend about it. He just had to sit back and watch me travel around the country in tiny skirts and revealing tops. He couldn't even attend the events because security always came with me on those trips.

It was tough for both of us. I'd be onstage at a club, shaking my booty and texting Hank in between songs. Then when I got back to my hotel I would call him and we'd talk until I fell asleep. We knew in our hearts how we felt about each other. Would I really be texting him from the club if I didn't love him? Of course not, and he knew it.

At times, however, I would do things that didn't really make it easier on him.

One night I was on my way to a party and a camera crew

from TMZ was outside the club when we arrived. I was in a good mood and knew I needed to act a certain way in front of the cameras, so when I got out of the car I pulled my shirt down and flashed them.

I called Hank and told him what I'd done right away, and he was so mad. He knew my party-girl behavior was part of the deal, but he thought flashing was going overboard. Plus, I had been in the car with a few of my guy friends, and he hated that that was how I was acting around guys I knew. He didn't want to start a fight because I was drunk and out at a club and I couldn't be seen getting upset on the phone, but he did stress that I could still be Kendra without showing my boobs to everyone.

He was right. I promised I wouldn't do it again.

Then, a few weeks later, I was out drinking again at some party I was paid to be at and I flashed the cameras again. This happened over and over, and every time I talked to Hank about it, I blamed someone else. I'd say my friends got me drunk and the paparazzi talked me into it. Or I blamed my friends for egging me on. I used every excuse in the book. He didn't want to hear any of them.

I don't know why I kept flashing. It reminded me a little of my drug days. Back then I would do a bunch of drugs, get caught by my mom or a friend who cared about me, and say that I wasn't going to do it again. But it was only a matter of time—sometimes as soon as a day later—before I was doing drugs again. I was having trouble juggling both lives. I didn't want to upset Hank, but as long as I was living at the Mansion my brain kicked into party-Kendra mode when I was out.

Not long after the TMZ flashing, I went to the Dominican Republic for an appearance and it happened again. I felt like I was in another world, and away from all the cameras, so I didn't think I would get caught. Also, I swear on my life that I had to do it. I'd built up this persona, and there were thousands of people at the club who wanted to see me, so I went up onstage and started dancing with some girl. The crowd wasn't that into it, so I grabbed the mike and began rapping on stage. That picked the crowd up a little, but then a guy screamed, "Flash your boobs!" and before I knew it the whole place was chanting, "Flash! Flash! Flash!"

I didn't want to do it. I even left the stage once without doing it. I knew it was wrong, and I knew Hank would be pissed. But even when I was offstage the crowd was still begging for some boobs. I felt the pressure . . .

Fuck it.

I went out there and gave them what they wanted. If it's going to make them happy, then I'll give them some boob. Why not? I pulled my shirt down and the crowd went wild. My work was done, so I ran off the stage and that was it . . . until, of course, the video showed up all over the Internet.

Hank was mad, and I swore that I wouldn't do it again. He was actually pretty calm and reasonable, considering I kept doing the one thing he hated the most. But at some point he had to break. That breaking point came when I went to Las Vegas to film the show and the producers wanted me to sky-dive topless. Okay, maybe I wanted to do it—maybe it was even my very scary idea—but for Hank's sake, let's just say someone forced me to do it.

Before I went I swore up and down that I wouldn't show my boobs—for real this time. I meant it.

I lied.

Again, he couldn't say much when I told him because he was in the car with someone and he couldn't be heard yelling at a girlfriend he supposedly didn't have. But even without getting into a real argument with him, I knew it was wrong. I'd broken a promise—a real promise—and I felt terrible.

Making fans or photographers happy wasn't worth feeling as horrible as I felt, but I was caught between wanting to change my ways and holding on to what got me there in the first place.

Although we didn't fight often, this was our ongoing battle. But fighting every now and then is a good thing, and Hank and I could always talk our arguments out. I listened to him and he listened to me. It made us better as individuals and stronger as a couple.

This time he was right. It was time for me to grow up and decide what was more important to me. If I was going to make this relationship work, I needed to make some sacrifices. Hank was certainly holding up his end of the bargain. Most guys wouldn't put up with a girl living the Playboy Mansion lifestyle, the long-distance relationship, and being forced to keep the whole thing a secret. He was so committed and so patient, and I knew he deserved better.

CHAPTER 18

The Secret to Love

By the time we were filming the fifth season of *The Girls Next Door*, I think Holly, Bridget, and I were just sort of going through the motions. Each girl knew exactly what she had to do to make an episode interesting, so we were able to get through shooting fairly quickly.

We all knew the show was nearing its end, so we wanted to leave a good lasting impression on the viewers. After all, we were pros.

Bridget was the creative, motherly type who was always fixing problems and making some artsy shit, but she was no pushover. If something went wrong or she didn't like what was happening in an episode she was the first to say "Fuck you" and get her way. She means business, and I think fans got that from her in the fifth season.

Holly was the nice, polite girl who had a smile on her face at all times, but she was also strong and courageous and never gave up. I've never seen Holly cry. You'd think I would be the toughest of the three of us, but I lost my shit a number of times. Holly was the fighter.

During the fifth season the producers wanted to film us taking a scuba-diving test, but Holly didn't know how to swim. We figured Holly would just sit this one out, but she had taken a few swimming lessons with Amanda Beard for a previous episode, and then, knowing we had the scuba episode coming up, she really worked at learning to swim off camera. She was determined to pass that test.

On the day we went out on the ocean to get certified, the water was really choppy. It was a terrible day for scuba diving. In the episode it looks like we all passed the test easily, but the truth is, none of us wanted to even get in the water, except Holly. Holly—who had just learned how to swim—was determined to get that certification, and she did it. It was amazing.

As for me, I was the resident party girl, but I was doing my best to put an end to that off camera. I didn't care how I looked on the show, but I wanted to prove to Hank how much he meant to me, and that meant toning it down in public. Plus, I missed Hank so much that it was hard for me to have fun the way I used to.

I began focusing all my energy on figuring out how Hank and I could meet up without getting caught. I was losing my mind without seeing him, and then, just before football season started, Hank told me he was going to Cabo San Lucas with some of his boys and he wanted me to come. I didn't really want to crash a boys' weekend, but at the same time I *totally* wanted to crash the boys' weekend. I didn't know how I was going to make it work, but I told Hank that I would find a way to see him.

At the time Hef was being way more lenient on the rules because he knew our time at the Mansion was almost up, but there was no way in hell he was just going to let me go to Cabo for no reason. So I found a reason. I had my publicist book me an appearance at a hotel down there so I could make it a work trip. It worked out perfectly—I even scored a free flight and a room at the ME Cabo Resort.

I took two girls with me so the trip seemed like a girls' weekend in addition to a work event, and of course Joe, the bodyguard, was there, too. I use the term *bodyguard* lightly. Joe was a skinny, gray-haired guy in his sixties—not exactly the ass-kicker you might imagine. He was more the guy who got me out of bed and to my event on time, and who stayed sober to make sure there was no funny business. Don't get me wrong—he always had my back, so in a sense he was a bodyguard, but in a more fatherly sort of way.

Joe and I had developed a good relationship, but he was super-loyal to Hef, so Hank and I knew we had to be sneaky—especially since he had seen Hank a couple of times already and was starting to get suspicious. Hank and I always said that we were family friends, and we never acted like we were together when Joe—or anyone else for that matter—was around. Plus, in Cabo there would be paparazzi, so we had to be extra careful.

Just being in Cabo with Hank made all the work I had to do to get there, and all the sneakiness that had to take place once we were there, worth it. The day we arrived I met all of his friends. We went off-roading on ATVs, and then we all went to the hotel pool, where I bought shots for everyone. I was like one of the guys, cracking on Hank and talking trash. I fit right in—they loved me.

My girls came out, too, and they met all of Hank's friends, but they also had one another to hang out with, so they weren't too concerned with what I was doing. That's why I took two friends: if you bring one, they count on you to be with them all the time; with two, they entertain each other. So they didn't care if I was off somewhere with Hank. I had everything figured out.

Joe watched us the whole time, but it all looked platonic, so there was nothing for him to report.

Later that first day, as soon as I saw an opening, I made an excuse and went to my room. Once Joe had gone to his room and all of our friends were good and drunk and looking for fun, Hank came and met me. Finally, we had some alone time.

Sitting on the balcony, looking out at the ocean and getting to be "us" for a change, felt so good. I felt so relaxed when we could let our hair down and be a real couple.

As we sat on the balcony talking, Hank told me he loved me for the first time.

Whaaaaaaat?!? I wasn't expecting that at all. I knew he loved me, and I loved him, but I was still shocked when he said it out loud. For some reason, hearing it totally caught me off guard. Maybe it was because he took the relationship to the next level so suddenly, or maybe I just didn't expect a guy to be so brave and just come out with it before knowing exactly what my reaction would be. Either way, I forget what my exact response was, but it definitely wasn't "I love you, too." Even though I'm sure he would have been more than happy to hear it then, I didn't want him to think I was saying it just because he'd said it to me, so I held out.

In the past I had dated guys for at least a year before I said "I love you." Hank and I had been dating a couple of months (and we really spent only a few days actually together), so this felt pretty quick. In general, dropping L-bombs doesn't come easy for me; loving someone and telling them you love them are two totally different things. Saying "I love you" is a very powerful thing to me. Some people say it all the time and don't think about it, but I save those words for when I mean them.

Even though he's not a perfect person, to me, Hank was perfect. He proved to me that he is not a typical cocky athlete. Everything that he said to me was truthful, and everything about him was real. There was never any bullshit with him. There were no ifs, ands, or buts about it—I loved him. I just needed a couple of days to catch my breath before I said it back.

A few days later Hank and I snuck off to go parasailing together. It was the first time we were able to get away from the group and Joe, and we were excited to do a public activity together, just the two of us. However, I was scared to death about floating in the air while tied to a moving boat, even though Hank would be there with me.

Right when we were about to go up I told him to hold on to me tightly. He wrapped his arms around me and told me not to worry. Seconds later we were soaring over the Pacific Ocean. It was incredible. With about five hundred feet of air between the ocean and us, I yelled for Hank to look me in the eyes.

He turned to me and I shouted, "I love you!"

In that moment we were both so happy. We knew how we felt about each other before the trip, but hearing and saying those words was really special.

Hank spent the night in my room, and the next day it was time to go back to our regular lives. He had training camp and I had a show to film. Just after the big "I love you" exchange, we were splitting up again. It was the hardest good-bye yet. I started crying as soon as I woke up because I didn't want to leave him.

While I sobbed uncontrollably and packed my bags, Hank stepped into the bathroom. A few minutes later the maids came in to clean. I was so upset that I forgot Hank and I weren't supposed to be caught in the same room, and seconds later Joe knocked on the door. I wiped away my tears as well as I could and let Joe inside. He'd come to make sure I was getting ready to leave, not to check up on me, but he'd unknowingly trapped Hank in the bathroom.

Joe was talking and talking and it didn't seem like he was going to leave until I left with him. Luckily the maids were there, and as they were making some noise and providing a distraction, Hank was able to peek out from the bathroom and find the perfect time to slip out without Joe seeing him. We didn't even get one last kiss or hug in. Hank just mouthed *I love you* and disappeared.

I cried the entire flight back. I opened up to my friends about our relationship and they did their best to comfort me, saying Hank and I looked perfect together and that someday it would all work out.

I knew that to make relationships work, you had to sacrifice, and that nothing in life comes easy, but this was getting too hard to handle. I was dying inside, and since Hank and I had left Cabo without any real plans to see each other again, I didn't have anything but loneliness to look forward to.

I thought it was going to be months before we saw each other, and I was miserable about it. Then a few days later, out of nowhere, my agent told me he'd booked me an appearance at Harrah's Hotel and Casino in Atlantic City during what was, coincidentally, Hank's bye week during the football season.

I was ecstatic. The only downside to the trip was that Joe would be there, watching over me yet again. If he saw Hank so soon after seeing him in Cabo he would definitely know something was up.

Plus, Bridget was coming on the trip, too, so I knew I was going to get busted. My only option was to tell Bridget about Hank and hope for the best. This was a good opportunity to test our friendship and see if she would rat me out. Also, I figured if I told her before she started asking Joe and me a bunch of questions like "Who is this guy?" and "Where is Kendra going?" just maybe it could work.

When we got to Atlantic City I sat her down in my hotel room and broke the news. "Listen," I said, slightly fearful of her reaction. "I met someone."

"You did," she said in a less surprised voice than I expected.

"I've been seeing him for a while," I told her. "And I love him."

"Wow," she said, sounding surprised now. "I had a feeling you maybe met someone, but 'love'—that's big."

"I know."

"What are you going to do?"

"I don't know."

There was a weird second or two of silence as Bridget collected her thoughts. Before she could say anything else, I told her a little bit about Hank and wrapped the conversation quickly so we could move on with our day. I was scared that she would run off and tell Hef, but I wasn't going to ask her to lie for me. At that point I was willing to roll the dice and see what happened.

Hank came to our appearance that night, and then back at the hotel, when Joe was out of sight, we kissed and held hands. It felt good to be a real couple in front of Bridget, who was forced to see our PDA since she and I were sharing a hotel suite. She thought we were cute, and she really liked Hank. It was important to me that she saw how great we were together because I didn't want her to think I was messing around just for fun. I was serious about this relationship and she picked up on that right away.

Joe picked up on it, too, but that didn't stop us.

Hank lived only an hour or so away from Atlantic City, and he really wanted me to see his apartment. After all that time I had never seen his place—and you can learn a lot about a guy by seeing his home. I really wanted to go.

We snuck out of the hotel in the middle of the night and drove to Philadelphia. Since he was a football player, I didn't expect the apartment to be very homey. I thought he'd have a big over-the-top place with a huge TV and not much else, but he actually had a comfortable and classy apartment. I could tell he was a very down-to-earth guy. He was also very organized;

everything was in its place, and his bed was made. He'd probably only made it because he knew I was coming, but I still
thought it said a lot about him. The best part was that I found
out he had a bunch of *Star Wars* toys, and Transformers—he
was a big kid. I thought that was so attractive.

Hank and I slept there that night and drove back to Atlantic
City at the crack of dawn so we could be in our separate rooms
before everyone woke up. Again, waking up and knowing we had
to say good-bye was tough. Again, I cried. We hugged for hours
this time, but I still didn't want to let go. And just in case, I left a
pair of my underwear in his apartment to mark my territory.

When I got back to the Mansion, Mary, Hef's assistant, called
me into her office. Joe had figured everything out and had told
her about Hank. He was worried that between Cabo and Atlantic City we might have been photographed together. We could
play the "family friend" card the first time, but if photos turned
up from both weekends, Hef and *Playboy* would come off looking bad.

Mary sat me down and asked me what was going on. She
was like a mom to all of us girls, and I loved her to death. There
was no way I could lie to her. So I told her the truth—sort of.
I said that I had met a guy and that I thought I wanted him to
be my boyfriend. That was close enough to the truth—and just
enough to get me kicked out of the Mansion.

Mary was sweet, and deep down she probably knew it was
only a matter of time before this happened. She wasn't mad at
me, but she did tell me that I had to tell Hef. I walked up to
Hef's room with my head held high, but I was nervous about
his reaction. I never wanted to disrespect Hef. He had done so

much for me, and I owed it to him to make sure I never made him look bad.

I knocked on his door and he invited me in. He was sitting on his bed looking through photos for the centerfold, and I hopped up next to him.

"I have something I need to tell you," I said, pushing some of the photos out of the way so he could focus.

"What's up, doll?" he replied.

"I met someone and I think I like him," I said, my voice cracking ever so slightly. "He's a really good guy. I think I want to start dating him."

"Okay," he said. "If that's what you want, then that's what we'll do."

He didn't have much else to say, but it seemed like he understood. In fact, he didn't act surprised at all. Maybe this happens all the time for him. Maybe there is a shelf life for all of his girlfriends. It was hard telling him, but in the end he was really cool about it.

We decided that I would keep things quiet for the remainder of the season, wrap *The Girls Next Door*, and then move out of the Mansion and on with my life.

It was such a relief that Hef knew. There was always this fear inside me that he'd find out and be mad—or worse, disappointed—so getting it off my chest was a huge relief. Plus, Hef let me fly out to see some of Hank's games and host events in Philly. There was no more sneaking into separate hotel rooms in the middle of the night or hiding in bathrooms. It was such a nice feeling to have some freedom.

When I was alone with Hank I wanted to prove I was wifey

material. I'd dust his apartment, light candles, and have a sandwich waiting for him when he got home from practice. I turned his place into our place. I even made him get rid of all of his old furniture because I didn't want to sit on a couch or lie in a bed that some other girl had been on.

In public, we still had to keep our relationship a secret. But after months of sneaking around and hiding things from Joe and the rest of the *Playboy* staff, Hank and I were pros.

On one hand, it was great that Hef finally knew what was going on, but on the other, I had just made a huge change in my life and there was no turning back. It all hit me one day and I freaked out.

Was I doing the right thing? I loved Hank, but I had just given up living in the Playboy Mansion and having a hit television show for him. Hef wasn't going to let me have both, and without a ring on my finger, I had just blindly chosen Hank. It was a huge risk, and I started worrying about it. A lot.

"You're not promised to me," I'd say to Hank. "What am I doing?"

"Don't worry," he'd reply calmly. "Everything will be okay. I love you, and it's all going to work out."

I knew I was ready to leave the Mansion, but I felt like I was leaving just for Hank. I didn't have a backup plan. I was putting all my eggs in one basket (or Baskett, in this case), and that scared the hell out of me. If Hank left me or cheated on me, I was totally screwed. I'd have nothing.

"Everything will work out," he'd say.

That wasn't enough for me. I needed to know where this was going.

He wanted me to just follow my heart and trust him, but that was not an easy thing for me to do. I brought up my fears over our future a lot and Hank got frustrated, especially when we could only talk about them over the phone; not being able to talk face-to-face because our relationship was still under wraps only made it more frustrating.

I was scared. I loved Hank with all my heart, and when we were sneaking around I'd dreamed about a day when we would be a happy couple out in the open. But now that that opportunity was close to becoming a reality, all I could think was, *What have I done?*

CHAPTER 19

On My Own Now

As it turned out, while I was busy bugging out about my decision to leave a hit TV show and life in paradise, Holly was also making some major changes in her life. Just as Hank and I had been sneaking around, Holly was secretly dating magician Criss Angel.

I was so wrapped up in my own world that I hadn't even taken the time to look around and see what the other girls were up to, and when she told me that she was moving on, too, I had mixed feelings.

On one hand, I thought it was cool that we were both going through the same thing at the same time, and I was thrilled that she considered me a good enough friend to confide in me. I had been worried that *I* would somehow ruin the show for everyone, but with Holly also on the move, it became more of a group decision. That made it a lot less stressful.

Her new romance was also good because it brought Holly

and me even closer together. I felt like we were on the same page, and we were in a position to go out and have some fun together as actual friends.

When she was with Hef she was very by-the-book. Everything she did was so carefully thought out, and she always followed every rule. You can't live your life like that. Some rules are meant to be broken; it's the only way to stay sane. But she was always Hef's number one, and she wanted to make sure everyone knew it, so she always did whatever she had to to live up to that status. She was like the First Lady. I don't know why it was so important to her to uphold that position, but she genuinely loved Hef and I think she needed people to know that, so she acted like a model girlfriend.

Once she met Criss, she did a complete one-eighty, and I think she changed in a very good way. She was more outgoing, acted more her age, and stopped caring what people thought of her.

The downside was that at one point Holly really thought she was going to spend the rest of her life with Hef, and he loved her, too, so it was a tough breakup for both of them.

When Hef didn't give her the relationship she wanted, she got really depressed. She was devoted to Hef and she cared a lot about *Playboy* as a whole. She was a total go-getter in life, especially with Hef. She had his heart; she knew what she wanted from him, and she usually got it.

But in the end it became apparent that it wasn't going to last, so she moved on.

Once word got out that she was seeing Criss, she sort of stopped trying to hide it, and it was hard to watch Hef go through that. She was hurt because he didn't give her the exclusive relationship she really wanted, so she went out and showed the world she was moving on.

By then everything about my relationship with Hank was out in the open and I saw Hef as a friend. We talked about everything and I could see that he was upset at the way everything was unfolding, but Holly was done. She'd checked out emotionally. She had spent years being a real girlfriend to Hef, taking care of him, making sure the magazine was classy, and doing everything perfectly, and once it was over it was over.

I admired her strength, but I still felt bad about the situation and made sure I was there for Hef as a friend until the day I left.

About my departure . . . I knew my time was almost up at the Mansion, but I didn't really have much of a plan for moving forward. I had a few meetings with networks about starring in my own show and I thought that could be a great opportunity, but nothing was definite yet and I wasn't sure if it was ever going to happen.

Plus, my old agent had once talked me into going into the top executives' offices at E!, demanding my own show. He showed up at the meeting dressed like a mobster and looked and acted like a fool, and they laughed in our faces. It was so embarrassing. After I fired him, I went in and apologized to the people at E! I shouldn't have listened to that guy, but it was my fault for following his lead. Luckily, after my apology we were back on good terms, and they were the obvious first choice for any new show I might do.

Every idea that was tossed around, though, was for some wild party-girl show or a dating show where I'd be out on the town looking for guys. Then the idea shifted to me living in a party house with a bunch of girls. Nothing seemed to synch with the new Kendra I was becoming. Word had started to spread about Hank and me dating, but no one realized how serious we were. Everyone assumed he was disposable, so every idea for a show was essentially all about sex.

I didn't know what to do. I ran the idea of pretending to be single just for a show by Hank, and as the words were coming out of my mouth I knew it was wrong. None of those shows were going to work for me. I realized I'd rather not be on television at all than pretend that I didn't love Hank.

But I needed to work, so I went to Kevin Burns, the executive producer of *The Girls Next Door*, who was working with me on coming up with a new show.

"Look, I have a boyfriend," I said. "Can he be involved in the show?"

"No," he answered quickly. "Who is this guy?"

"He's important to me."

"Nobody wants to see you with a boyfriend. It's going to be a hard sell."

"What if the show is based around me being on my own and starting a life with him?"

"Tell me more."

I sort of just volunteered Hank to be in my show, which was not even a real show yet. When I mentioned this to Hank he wasn't thrilled about it. It was certainly better than my pretending to be single, but Hank had his own career and wasn't sure being on TV was for him. He's not a public guy, so I knew it would be a stretch, but it seemed to me like the only way for it to work and for us to be together.

After laying down some ground rules—no sexual stuff, no making anyone look like a fool—Hank agreed to give it a shot. Kevin still looked at Hank like he was a nerd, but he agreed to put him in the pilot. We thought maybe Hank would just sort of show up in an episode every now and then, but when the people at E! saw the pilot they loved him.

Nothing was definite, though, and no deal was set. Time was ticking and I didn't have a new show locked in. I didn't even have Hank locked in. We were a couple, and we were happy, but I had no clue what the future held for us. I didn't want to pressure him into anything, but it was tough to keep my emotions in check.

Then, even though we were still doing our best to hide the relationship, more and more people were starting to find out about us. I was going to games in Philadelphia and sitting with the coach's wife instead of in the players' wives' section in order to not get caught, but it didn't work. People were starting to put it all together.

The nail in the coffin, so to speak, came when I was in Philly visiting Hank in the middle of football season. We were out with some friends, who happened to have just gotten engaged, and I took a second to try on the girl's ring. Not only did it look great on me and probably put all kinds of pressure on Hank, but people in the bar saw Hank and me kissing and me with a ring on and jumped to conclusions. Before I knew it, it was all over the Internet that I was engaged.

Hell, no. I was not going to let other people decide my future.

I denied everything, even the relationship, because I wasn't going to be pressured into admitting anything about Hank or hurting Hef in any way. Things eventually died down, but I felt awful about all the unwanted exposure.

After trying to lie low for a bit, on Halloween weekend I hosted a big party in San Diego. I got pretty drunk, which was not smart because I had to fly out early the next morning with my family to Seattle to meet Hank, who was in town playing the Seahawks, and his family. I didn't know why the hell he wanted to turn a game in Seattle into some big family vacation, but I wasn't going to argue.

I arrived on Saturday, groggy and hungover, and all I wanted to do was sleep, but our families were dying to be tourists and check out the Space Needle. I actually thought it would be a pretty cool thing to do, if I wasn't so tired.

"Rest up," Hank told me when I got to our hotel room. "When I get back from our team meeting we are going to the Space Needle."

"Nooo, Hank," I whined. "I'm too tired."

"It will be fun."

"If you want me to get out of this bed, you might have to propose to me," I said, totally joking.

He didn't say anything. I was kidding around, obviously. Maybe he just didn't think that was funny?

Hank left for his meeting, so I was able to rest a little bit. But after what felt like ten seconds of sleep he was back, waking me up and urging me to get dressed.

"I'm tired, baby," I moaned, desperately wanting to stay in bed.

"Come on, it's time to go," he said. "Our families are waiting."

"Look at the weather," I argued with one eye open to peek out the window. "The Needle is going to be closed."

I didn't even know if that made sense, but I was willing to try anything to get him to let me sleep.

"Get up! Get up! Get up!"

"Ahhhh, *fine!*"

I got up slowly and got dressed while Hank did every-thing possible to speed me up. *What is wrong with this guy?* I thought.

We went downstairs and packed into a car—me, my mom, my brother, Hank, and his mom and dad. We were like the Gris-wolds in those National Lampoon's *Vacation* movies, heading to the big, fancy Space Needle.

When we got to the top it was windy and rainy but Hank was so into it. Actually, when I looked around I thought it was a pretty romantic place, but after all my complaining I wasn't about to let anyone know that I was having a good time. Eagles TV happened to be filming a segment up there for their pre-game show, but this was purely a tourist trip for us. Hank didn't have to do an interview, and I sure as hell didn't have any plans to get in front of a camera, but just as we were about to leave Hank decided he wanted us all to take a nice family photo. So we all lined up, and before the shot was taken, Hank popped out of the line and dropped to one knee in front of me.

I looked around and saw everyone in my family looking at me, teary-eyed. I couldn't believe what was happening. In my head I was thinking, *Are you fucking serious right now?* I thought it was a joke.

Hank looked me in the eyes and said, "Over the past seven

months I've gotten to know you, and . . ." I think I blacked out a little because it was all a blur to me from then on. Luckily one of our moms pulled Eagles TV over to film everything and capture the moment.

He pulled a ladybug-shaped box that I'd told him I loved way back when we went together to the Del Mar Fair from his pocket. That day I had told him about the ladybugs I found when my mom took me to the bay after my dad left. He'd asked his brother, who was at the fair with us, to buy the box for him when I wasn't paying attention.

Hank had bought the box—and, it turned out, the ring— before I freaked out about telling Hef, before I pressured him about our future, before pretty much everything. There had never been any reason to worry. He knew he wanted to marry me from the very beginning.

"Will you marry me?" Hank asked.

In the most serious voice I have ever used I immediately gave him my response: "Yes, I will marry you."

We kissed and hugged, and I spent the rest of the day staring at the ring on my finger and bouncing off the walls with excitement. I couldn't believe I was engaged.

When I was able to think clearly again, I called Mary and told her the news; I knew it was only a matter of time before it got out. I was so happy, and she was happy for me. Hef and everyone at *Playboy* loved it, too. They couldn't believe that the crazy little tomboy party-girl was now engaged. Their baby was all grown up.

The next day we went to Hank's game, and then we had to go our separate ways again. That really sucked.

It was strange going back to the Mansion as an engaged woman. (I'm sure that doesn't happen at the Playboy Mansion very often.) We were still filming the show and doing photo shoots, and I had to take the ring off every time I was around the cameras. I was so happy to be engaged that I hated taking it off, but it had to be done.

Finally we finished filming, and then I spent a couple of weeks packing up my life at the Mansion and preparing to move forward.

During one of my last days at the Mansion I took a break from packing my belongings and went in to Mary's office to see what she was up to. We started talking about Hank and my wedding and, half kidding, I said, "Wouldn't it be cool if I got married at the Mansion?"

I was only *half* kidding because I really did think it would be an incredible place to get married, but I also thought there was no way it was ever going to happen. To my surprise, Mary liked the idea. She said she was going to ask Hef, and I figured she meant in a few weeks, after I had left the Mansion—or at the very least after I had left the room. But Hef walked in a minute or two later, and the first thing out of her mouth was, "What do you think about Kendra getting married here?"

"Shut up!" I yelled, my face turning bright red. I ran up to my room.

Hef followed me and sat down next to me on my bed and said, "If you want to get married here, I'd love it."

"Oh my God!" I replied.

I couldn't believe it. The only wedding that had ever been held at the Playboy Mansion was Hef's own wedding, back in the eighties. It really was an honor for him to allow us to get married there.

"Are you serious?" I asked again, just to make sure.

"Of course, darling."

"Thank you so much," I said. "Let me ask Hank."

"The offer is there," Hef said before leaving my room. "Let me know what you decide."

It was certainly something to think about.

When the time came for me to move, I was way more emotional than I thought I would be. The scene in the show where they filmed me saying good-bye to Hef, the girls, and the staff was the most genuine scene I ever shot. Those were real tears.

I'm terrible with good-byes; I usually just make them quick and hide behind a tough face the entire time. But for the show I had to stick around, and the tears came pouring down. Hef, Holly, and Bridget were and always will be a huge part of my life, and we'd been through a lot together.

When the cameras stopped rolling I went back and said good-bye to everyone again. I wanted them to know I was really going to miss them and that I wasn't putting on an act for the show.

I saw these people every day of my life for nearly five years, and while they all hold a special place in my heart, I knew I wouldn't be seeing them very much in the future. Moving out felt like a graduation of some sort. I was happy to be moving on to a new adventure, but sad about all I was leaving behind. It was definitely a bittersweet moment.

I packed a couple of bags and my dogs into my car and drove to my new town house in the Valley in the pouring rain. The movers had to start loading everything—electronics, memorabilia, and bags and bags of clothes—into my home that night because I had to be settled before starting my new show, which had been officially picked up and was ready to roll.

I got to my new place and at nine o'clock at night I realized, *Oh, shit, I don't have any furniture.*

Everything in the Mansion was property of *Playboy*, so all I had were clothes and the crap I'd accumulated while living at the Mansion (I was a real hoarder back then). I ran to a furniture store that was open late and bought a couch and a bed and everything I needed as quickly as possible. The only problem was that they couldn't deliver any of it until the next day.

I didn't know what to do. I had just said all my big good-byes, and I was excited about my new life. Hank and I were engaged and ready to plan a wedding and film all the fun for a new show. Going back, even for a day, seemed strange.

But everyone at the Mansion was like family to me, and I was stuck. I called Hef and he immediately invited me back. Who says you can never go home again?

I went back to the Mansion, spent one last night in my old room, and then moved out for good. My final good-bye was a big step for me. You usually don't recognize a life-changing moment as it is happening, but walking out that door—again—I knew that nothing would ever be the same. (For real this time!) In that moment I felt like I was growing up, which was both exciting and scary at the same time.

CHAPTER 20

A Biscuit in Mrs. Baskett

From the second I left the Mansion I was busy planning the wedding. We wanted to get married in June, so that gave us less than seven months to pull the whole thing together.

When I first told Hank about possibly having our wedding at the Playboy Mansion, I could tell he had some doubts. He hadn't met Hef yet, and he thought it would be strange to get married at my ex-boyfriend's house. While I really didn't consider Hef my ex-boyfriend, we had enough of a relationship that it was hard to argue with Hank. Beyond that, though, Hank wanted our life as a couple to start new and fresh, and having the wedding at the Mansion reminded him too much of my old life.

I was a little bummed because the Mansion is so beautiful and it meant a lot to me. It symbolized who I was and how I had grown up over the years. But I understood where Hank was coming from.

We went back and forth on what kind of wedding we wanted to have. Some days we'd decide we wanted a big wedding, and other times we were ready to run to the courthouse and just get it over with.

The one thing we knew was that we were ready to get hitched. After all the sneaking around and long-distance dating came to an end, we were relieved to be able to start a regular relationship. When football season was finally over and Hank and I could wake up next to each other every morning, it was such a great feeling that we just wanted to be married right away.

To that end, a quick wedding at the courthouse seemed like the easiest option, but Hank is a traditional kind of guy, and he thought we deserved a day to remember. As always, he was right.

Then we thought about having a destination wedding in Hawaii, but we knew that would be an expensive trip for our guests. We had no idea what we were going to do, until my mom stepped in.

"Kendra, who gets to have their wedding at the Playboy Mansion?" asked the woman who'd once told me to fear the orgy. "It's a beautiful place. You'd be making history. What's better than that?"

She was right. I went back to Hank and pleaded my case for a Mansion wedding, and he eventually changed his mind. The one condition, which we both agreed on, was that it was going to be our party, with our friends and family—not a *Playboy* party with naked chicks in the grotto.

Hef agreed, and Hank and I were getting married at the Playboy Mansion.

Once the venue was set, finding the right dress moved to the top of my priority list. I wanted to look hot! A few top designers offered to make me dresses. It was cool that these big-name people wanted to be involved, but deep down I didn't really think I was a designer-dress kind of girl.

One day I was walking down Ventura Boulevard in the Valley, and I passed a store called R-Mine Bridal. I decided to go in. My brain was wrapped around the wedding pretty tight, so whenever I had the opportunity to check out something wedding-related I jumped at the chance. The dresses were okay, but nothing really caught my eye, so I left and checked out a few other places.

A couple of weeks later I went back to R-Mine. The saleswomen there were so nice, and the store was so cute that I just figured I would swing by one more time. I was starting to get a little stressed out about how I didn't know what I wanted when I began talking to the owner, Armine. She gave me the best news ever: "You don't have to pick one of these dresses," she said. "You can design any dress you want."

Any dress I want? Now we're talking!

I liked that idea, and I liked working with a smaller shop rather than some big high-end place. I like to see people grow and I would rather work with a company on the rise than with someone who is already big-time.

R-Mine was my style, and now that I could design anything I wanted, the dress would be, too. The scary part was that my whole wedding was now in *Playboy*'s and Armine's hands.

I quickly began to drive Armine insane. First I wanted jewels everywhere, and then I changed my mind and didn't want any jewels. I'd pop in all the time and ask, "So what's new with the dress?"

"Kendra, you just came in yesterday," she would say. "Nothing is new with the dress."

Luckily, while I was making Armine nuts, other than the early wedding madness, life with Hank was great. I loved living with him. Hank spent time with my dogs, which he hadn't done before, since I usually visited him. Martini loved him, but Raskal didn't like him at all at first. He's very protective of me, and he would growl whenever Hank came near me. But eventually they warmed up to each other, and now Hank gets along great with both dogs, which was important to me.

I also learned that Hank wakes up really early. Even in the off-season he is up at six A.M. and ready to work out. I sleep until at least ten A.M., so he gets to walk the dogs and make me breakfast. Yeah, I was pretty sure that this was going to work out really well.

In April, just a couple of months before the wedding, Hank and I went down to Clovis, New Mexico—Hank's hometown— for his charity golf tournament benefitting the Oasis Children's Advocacy Center. The center helps rehabilitate abused children, and Hank's dad has worked there for years.

It's a great charity event, and I was looking forward to seeing Hank's family and having fun with his friends. The only problem was that I was late—and not late as in the way I was always late for parties or massage therapy class. I was late, as in I should have gotten my period three weeks earlier.

During our layover on the way down, I took about ten pregnancy tests. They all came back negative, but I knew something was up. I was never late, and I was feeling nauseous, too. Eventually I convinced myself that the terrible feeling in my stomach was from the flight and tried to forget about it.

We had flown from Southern California to Dallas, where we were supposed to catch a small plane to Lubbock, which is about a two-and-a-half-hour drive to Clovis. But due to tornados we were forced to land in Amarillo. While Hank and I were devising a plan for how to get to Clovis, I started digging through my bags and discovered that I had one more pregnancy test left.

That should kill a few minutes. Why not take another one? I thought.

I went into the bathroom and took the test, and when I came out, Hank could tell the result by the look of fear on my face.

I was pregnant.

We always knew we wanted to have kids, but, um, not quite so soon. I had the new show starting, appearances to make, and a body that paid the bills. Plus, we weren't even married yet.

For about ten minutes we sat there in shock and didn't say one word to each other. I got stressed out and started crying. It was weird, though, because I was nervous and confused and a little bit happy all at the same time.

We decided to take a cab to a tiny hotel in town—which looked like a set from a western movie, by the way—and wait for Hank's parents to pick us up in the morning. Once we got to the hotel all the symptoms of pregnancy hit me like a ton of bricks. I was so emotional—crying (again), then laughing; excited one minute and freaked out the next—and after my outburst I became very hungry.

It was pouring rain, the wind was gusting, we were stranded at the hotel without a car, and it was nearly two A.M. but I needed food. Hank, being a true gentleman, walked to a Waffle House a mile away. He came back soaking wet with eggs, bacon, and grits. I was so happy I could have cried. Actually, I probably did.

Once I had a full stomach I was able to think straight. Hank and I were in a loving relationship, we were about to get married, and we could afford to have a baby. What was there to worry about? We kissed and hugged and fell asleep as a happy couple, ready to have a child.

The next morning Hank's parents picked us up and we headed to Clovis. At first we didn't know if we should tell them. Hank wanted to, but I didn't think I was ready. Throughout the whole two-hour drive, Hank, who was behind the wheel, kept looking at me in the mirror and giving me eyes that said, *Can I tell them?*

I kept shaking my head no, and his look turned to disappointment.

I wanted to wait at least until I went to see a doctor.

Hank had different plans.

"Mom, Dad, we have something to tell you."

Oh, boy, here we go.

"Kendra and I are going to have a baby."

His mom screamed, "Oh my God!" and his dad lifted his face from the newspaper he was reading and uttered a fairly calm "Wow, congratulations," before going back to his paper. Both of them were supportive, and it was a relief to know they were with us on this next step. His mom was ready to make baby blankets and everything.

The rest of the weekend I continued to experience every pregnancy symptom in the book as Hank's mom followed me around, asking me if I was okay every few minutes. While on the outside I probably looked like I was a mess, on the inside I was happy. I was going to have a baby, and his family was on board.

Now all I had to worry about was my family.

While the cameras weren't rolling on this trip, they did film another visit to New Mexico, and from that point on pretty much every experience I had as I prepared for my wedding day was caught on tape.

As soon as I got back from Clovis, I told the producers of the show that I was pregnant so they could plan their filming accordingly. They were happy for me, and I think they also enjoyed the extra drama it would add to the first season. Case in point: when I told them that my mom didn't yet know about my pregnancy, they asked if they could film me telling her.

Sometimes I thought the show actually took some pressure off of me. My mom tended to react to things I did more calmly because she didn't want to look bad on camera. I figured if I told her I was pregnant on the show, she might be shocked, but she wouldn't really be able to get mad. Seemed like a plan to me.

Bridget, who was really good at planning things, put together a bridal shower for me at my mom's house. She planned the party for Mother's Day weekend, which really seemed like the perfect time for me to break the news to my mom. My goal was to tell her in private before the cameras started rolling so she didn't feel totally ambushed, but the opportunity never came up.

The big moment arrived, and with the cameras pointing right at us I said that I couldn't drink Champagne . . . because I was pregnant.

My mom went completely insane. She stormed out of the party. Her reaction made me angry, so I stormed out, too, and got in my car and drove off.

I was really upset. Hank's parents had been so nice and understanding when they found out. How could my mom just desert me like that? What kind of mother was she?

Once I calmed down—and the cameras were far away—I went to her house to talk to her.

"I'm sorry I told you like that, in front of everyone," I said.

"How dare you set me up like that?" she replied.

"I know, I'm sorry. They wanted your real reaction. It was a stupid idea."

Then things took a turn for the worse. Still livid, she started going off about Hank and how I hadn't even known him that long and how she wasn't sure why I was even getting married so quickly.

Hold up, I thought.

"I love Hank," I argued. "I wouldn't be doing any of this if we didn't love each other."

"I thought this was your time to be strong and independent," she said. "I just don't know why you're making these decisions."

I was confused about what she was getting at, but I knew I didn't like it. I quickly took back my apology and left.

The next day we had to shoot a Mother's Day brunch, which the producers had set up at the Loews Hotel on the bay. As soon as my mom, my grandmother, my brother, and I were all there you could feel the tension in the room. I tried breaking the ice by pointing out the nice flowers that made up the centerpieces and telling my mom how much I liked her outfit. It didn't work.

Finally, I got frustrated. It was Mother's Day, damn it! I was having a baby and my family should be happy for me.

"Raise your hand if you are in favor of my life," I stood up and said.

No hands went up. They all just looked away.

I went off. I started yelling and screaming that nobody supported me even though I was doing so much for the family these days. I asked my mom in front of everyone—even the cameramen—if she was just mad because I hadn't given her money in a while.

Yikes, was that a bad move. She obviously wasn't thinking about money. I get that now; I also realize that she married young, had two kids, then had her heart broken, and she didn't want to see the same thing happen to me. But I was so furious at the time that I didn't see any of that.

The yelling went back and forth, and in the course of the family meltdown my grandmother even told me that I took after my father. She might as well have jabbed a knife into my heart. I was crushed.

No one was considering my side or the fact that just because that had all happened to my mom didn't mean it was going to happen to me. Hank and I loved each other, and they needed to trust that. They needed to trust me.

That whole day was filmed, but no part of it ever aired. It was way too intense for TV.

A couple of weeks went by and I still wasn't talking to my family and the wedding was around the corner. We were two weeks from the big day and Hank, who was back on the East Coast, called me up belligerent and drunk as hell and started yelling and cursing at me. We had been fighting over wedding details, and maybe there were some pre-wedding jitters, but his drunk ass called while I was hanging out with my friend Mykelle—a producer on *The Girls Next Door*—and just went off. I was so mad, I threw my ring off and chucked my phone in the toilet and in my head canceled the wedding.

I was crying hysterically and Mykelle called my mom for help. Despite everything we were going through, my mom came to the rescue, calmed me down, and made me go pick up that ring. She was right; this wedding was going to be great, and Hank was just drunk (which is funny, because he rarely drinks) and didn't mean what he said.

My mom and I made up, and Hank and I did the same. Everything was coming together. We even filmed a reenactment of my mom and me making up for the show, so everything could tie together nicely.

We couldn't live in the past. We had to rally and focus because the big day was around the corner.

I wanted to be really hands-on when it came to planning my wedding. I didn't want to just hire a stranger to handle all the details, so even though I had hired a wedding planner, leading up to the big day, I was still working the phones and dealing with all sorts of issues.

There were a lot of cooks in the kitchen, and it was actually kind of difficult to manage everyone. I had *Playboy*, the show, the wedding planner, the photographer, the florist, and so many other people involved, and we all had to be on the same page. The pregnancy hormones were definitely taking over, and coordinating everything with all those people drove me crazy.

But my biggest problem was the dress. Designing a wedding dress isn't easy. It's especially difficult when you want it to be form-fitting and your pregnant belly is growing bigger by the second.

I wasn't pregnant when I first told Armine she could design the dress, and when she measured me to fit everything perfectly tight to my body she said, "Oh my god, you're so small."

A couple of months later I was pregnant, but no one was supposed to know. I didn't know if I could trust her not to tell anyone, so I had to keep it a secret from her. I had to just roll the dice and hope she didn't notice. I had a million fittings, and every time I went in and put the dress on I looked like I was about to explode out of it.

One day Armine said, "Girl, you need to stop partying. Are you drinking too much right now?"

"No, I'm not drinking!" I said.

She could tell something was up. I was running to the bathroom every two minutes, and the dress was getting tighter and tighter.

My boobs started growing first, and she had to adjust the bodice multiple times. She kept saying, "Kendra you need to watch your weight." For a long time I just let her think I was getting fat, but I was starting to get nervous about the dress. A month before the wedding I had to tell her. It was obvious anyway, but we needed to get everything out in the open if my dress was going to fit on my wedding day.

"Look, I'm pregnant," I said.

"Oh my God, I knew it!" she yelled. "You're getting so much bigger. Your boobs are humongous!"

"Sorry I didn't tell you," I said.

"It's okay, but we're going to have to do something, because this dress isn't fitting."

She didn't tell me until later, but the week before the wedding she redid the entire dress. I am so grateful that she did. I wanted my dress to be tight, to show off my curves, and without telling me she somehow redid it and made it perfect. It was exactly what I wanted—an old-fashioned, curvy corset with a skirt that poofed out.

The wedding day arrived and everything was perfect. My dress fit right and the Mansion looked beautiful. It really is the most perfect destination for a wedding; it's so romantic, and it looks like a castle. I had never dreamed of a fairytale wedding—I never really dreamed of a wedding at all—but I got one. It was absolutely magical.

Before the guests arrived, I walked all around the grounds and thought, *Wow, this is even better than I pictured.*

When all the guests were seated and Hank was standing at the altar waiting for me to walk down the aisle, I peeked out a window to see how he looked. He appeared to be really happy. Sometimes the groom looks scared to death, like he thinks he's about to make some big mistake. Hank didn't have that look. Thank God!

Holly and Bridget were two of my seven bridesmaids, and they walked down the aisle first. I loved having them as part of my wedding party. We went through so much together, it felt right that they were part of the ceremony.

Then it was my turn to walk down the aisle.

I had blurted out in an interview a few months before the wedding that I thought it would be cool for Hef to walk me down the aisle, but after Hank and I thought about it, we realized it would be a better honor for my brother, Colin, to have.

He deserved it. He learned a lot from my mistakes as a kid but he also went through his own rough phase. There were times when he veered off-course and ran with bad crowds, but in the end he worked his way back to the right path. He was an independent guy who never cared what other people thought about him—I'd like to think he learned that from me—and I would try to talk to him when times were tough, but we didn't always have a strong bond and I know he didn't enjoy hearing lectures from me.

But now we had a better relationship than I'd ever imagined, and I didn't want anyone else to walk me down the aisle.

Leading up to the wedding, I thought about my dad a couple of times. As I was putting all the details together, I wondered what he was thinking. I had heard that he had inherited a bunch of money a couple years back and moved to Costa Rica, but surely he must have known his daughter was getting married. I wondered if he cared, or if he regretted missing out on the biggest day of my life. But on the day of my wedding he didn't cross my mind once. Just like during all the other events in my life, he wasn't there, and that seemed more normal to me than any other scenario. I had the greatest kid in the whole world on my arm as I walked down the aisle, and that felt right.

As anyone who watched the wedding episode of *Kendra* saw, I of course screwed up the words I was supposed to repeat after the minister. I wish I could say that I did that just for the cameras, but it was real. I have the worst memory ever.

But that was all right. Nothing was going to ruin my perfect day.

Eventually we got the "I do's" out and, for better or worse, richer or poorer, in sickness and in health, I was Mrs. Hank Baskett and he was, um, Mr. Kendra Wilkinson—'til death do us part.

Walking through the Mansion and out the back door and into the party as a married couple for the first time, with everyone cheering for us, was such a happy moment. That walk felt like it was in slow motion, and I was so proud to be Hank's wife.

Hank and I danced for the first time as husband and wife to George Strait's "I Cross My Heart," the song that we'd danced to in the hotel room on our very first weekend away together. From the minute he started twirling me around, I knew that would forever be our song. It was a special moment, and I'm pretty sure I even saw some big football players tear up as they watched us.

The second dance went to Hef. By the time the wedding rolled around, Hank had gotten to know Hef really well, and he understood our relationship. Whether I decided to call him an old boyfriend or a father figure or even just a friend, the title didn't matter; Hef cared for me when few others did, and he believed in me when I barely believed in myself. On my wedding day I think it's safe to say that of all people, Hef was the most proud.

We danced to his favorite song, "As Time Goes By," from *Casablanca*—the movie we watched on one of my first nights at the Mansion. Every time he put on an old black-and-white movie I dreaded watching it. I would walk into the movie room and nine times out of ten the second the lights went out I would sneak out the back. But every time I stayed I loved the movie.

Then Hank danced with his mom to "A Song for Mama" by Boyz II Men. He's a big mama's boy, and I love that about him.

The rest of the night was a ton of fun. I ate, danced, drank Martinelli's apple juice, and smiled. I couldn't have asked for a better day, and my fairy-tale wedding at the Mansion was a perfect end to that part of my life, and also the perfect way to start a lifetime of new beginnings.

The second Hank and I got in the limo to go to our hotel suite (the first time we were alone all night), I said, "Let's fuck" . . . and we did, right there in the back of the limo. Now *that's* the perfect way to start a lifetime of new beginnings!

CHAPTER 21

The Adventure Continues

After the wedding there was little time for Hank and me to relax and enjoy being newlyweds. We were busy filming the final episodes for the new show and then, before we could even catch our breath after we wrapped, it was time for football season.

After fighting through a long-distance relationship with Hank when I lived in the Playboy Mansion there was no way I was going through it again, especially since we were expecting a baby. That meant it was time to pick up and move again.

I was barely moved into my L.A. town house before I started packing my belongings to move to Hank's home outside Philadelphia.

Since football season had already started, I didn't have much help from Hank. I was five months pregnant and packing boxes while yelling at moving men who didn't speak English to watch out for my breakables. There were a lot of expensive wedding gifts in those boxes—engraved keepsakes and champagne glasses.

I heard things breaking and lost my mind.

"Oh my God, be careful," I yelled, but in a nice way. "You can break this one, but don't you dare touch my pimp cups!"

I don't think they understood.

I got a pimp cup once from Don "Magic" Juan. That pimp cup is my baby. It's from a real pimp, so I didn't want it to break.

Como se dice "pimp cup" en Español?

Freaked out, I called my mom. "Just let them do their job," she said. "Everything will be fine."

She's very trusting. Me, I worry. I wanted to see every step they took so I was absolutely sure my valuables—including that pimp cup—arrived to my new home in one piece.

I was putting a lot of pressure on this move. It was a big deal for me to head to the East Coast, away from my friends and family, to be by Hank's side, even though he would be traveling a lot for games and busy most of the time when he was home.

Good friends are hard to find these days, and I realized that even more when I got to Philly. Living in a new city, with new people, was overwhelming. I got very lonely, and when I would leave the house to pick up food or run errands, I felt like everyone was staring at me. In L.A., people recognized me from TV, but everyone is recognizable there so it's not as big of a deal. Now I went out and I couldn't handle it. If I was at the grocery store and accidentally dropped an orange I felt like everyone in town would be talking about it.

Don't get me wrong, I love the show and I love the fans, but sometimes I forget how to just be me. I used to be the life of the party, but I was quickly becoming more of a stay-in-and-watch-a-movie kind of girl, and developing a little bit of a phobia about leaving my house.

Being pregnant didn't help. It affected my mood, made me paranoid about everything, and pissed me off every time I struggled to just get off the couch.

I found a good doctor in the area and went for regular checkups. When she would go anywhere near my belly button, I would freak out. I hate my belly button! I couldn't look at it, especially when I was pregnant. Nobody can touch it. Even the words *belly button* give me the chills. Hank would joke that my belly button must be really dirty because I won't go near it.

This weird belly-button thing started when I was a kid and I saw a *Ren and Stimpy* episode where they went inside a belly button. After seeing that I had a huge fear of them, so when the doctor did an ultrasound I asked her to stay away from the button. Actually, I probably didn't ask—I probably told her in a stern voice.

I get loud and forceful sometimes, but when I was pregnant I was more demanding than usual. One night I went out to dinner with Hank and we got in a huge fight over Obama. I told him I liked Obama, but that I didn't understand all the hype because it didn't seem like he had done anything to change the country yet. He tried to change my opinion, and that's a big no-no. We were yelling back and forth, while the whole restaurant was watching. "You will never change my fucking opinion," I yelled. And I meant it. (Don't get me started on O.J., or whether Michael Jackson touched those little boys. We will fight about that all day. No one can change my mind, except for maybe Nancy Grace. I love Nancy Grace.) Add some crazy hormones to my stubbornness, my weird fear of belly buttons, and the fact that I'm a Gemini, and you can imagine the kind of fun Hank and I had during the pregnancy.

To make matters worse, just when I had the Philly house looking the way I wanted it to, Hank got cut from the team and signed by the Indianapolis Colts.

For a few days it was scary because we didn't know where we were going to end up. The Colts were an amazing team, though, so when that final decision came, I was pretty happy. I *did* have a say in where we went. Trust me—at that point no one was telling *me* where I had to move.

Hank had to leave right away, so I was alone in Philly without knowing anyone but my doctor. I didn't know where we were going to live or who my new doctor was going to be, but I couldn't stay alone and figure it out, so I hauled my seven-month-pregnant ass to Indy, where we stayed in a hotel for two weeks while we got settled.

We moved quickly, found a doctor, got to enjoy Indianapolis—which is a fantastic city, by the way—and settled into yet another new home just in time for me to have the baby.

I went in for an emergency C-section on the morning of December 10, because little Hank's head was too damn big and I didn't want my vagina all tore up like that. Nearly eighteen hours of eating ice chips and yelling at people later, I gave birth to Hank Jr., at 12:37 A.M. on December 11, 2009.

It was the happiest moment of my life, and Hank and our entire family were by my side the whole time. That's what made it the most special for me. Here I was, bringing a new life into this world, and I was surrounded by the people I love. There was a time when I thought I could never have such a strong support group, but when I was holding the baby I looked out at my mom, grandma, brother, Hank, and his parents and cried tears of joy at what an amazing family I was bringing this baby into.

The whole time I rarely thought about my dad. I was so happy enjoying what I had that I wasn't going to dwell on what I didn't have. Yeah, he popped into my mind a few times, but mainly I thought it was him who was missing out and not vice versa.

But when I was out of the hospital and back at the house, Colin, who had recently reconnected with him for reasons I'll never understand, told me that our father tried to send flowers to the hospital.

Tried? Who tries to send flowers and fails? *Don't bullshit me*, I thought. Who did he think he was trying to lie to like that?

I knew then that he would never again be a part of my life, and I would never let him get close to Hank Jr. I didn't care about my feelings so much, but if I let him back, I would always be just waiting for him to take off again. There will never be a day where my baby is in a position to ask, "Where's grandpa?" I wouldn't do that to him.

It is amazing how quickly those motherly instincts kicked in. He wasn't even a week old, and I was already protecting him from the world. That's the kind of mother I want to be. I want to help him when he falls, but I also want to let him explore the world around him, get his knees scraped up, and discover life on his own. My mom was a little too protective, so I ended breaking all the rules. (Although if not for her I'm not so sure I'd have the confidence to be a good mom in the first place, because through all the tough times, she gave me my backbone.) But I do think there is a happy medium where he can be loved and free to make some mistakes in life and learn to bounce back. Hank and I together (he can do the yelling) think we can do a good job and mold Hank Jr. into a great boy.

While he's an infant, though, I'm watching his every move. A couple of weeks after giving birth it was back to work for me, but everyone knew that Hank Jr. came first. Me, Hank, the show, my agent, my publicist—we all answered to the baby. If he got a cold or something, that was it—I wasn't leaving his side to promote the show or do anything.

I also wasn't going to rush to the gym when I had diapers to change and a body that wasn't ready. My agent, who clearly doesn't understand the female body, started immediately booking me for magazine covers and "body after baby" photo shoots.

"Already?" I asked him when he called with the news. "You've got to be kidding. I hope they are ready to airbrush the hell out of me."

Regardless of how little I wanted to do outside of caring for Hank Jr., life had to go on, especially when the Indianapolis Colts made it to the Super Bowl. It was a big deal for Hank, professionally, and I was excited to get to some warm weather, since the Super Bowl was being held in Miami. But with the baby, it was not business as usual. It was stressful packing everything— diapers, food, boogie-suckers—and flying with the baby for the first time. He was an angel and didn't cry once, but between the plane and the buses and the walking there was a lot of traveling. And in between all of that movement, he was busy eating and pooping.

Then I hosted a pre–Super Bowl party at a Miami nightclub and my world was turned upside down. I had hosted these events hundreds of times, but this felt different. I didn't know what to say or how to act. I used to grab the microphone and say, "What's up, motherfuckers? Let's get drunk tonight!" but I couldn't say that anymore. So at this party I was like, "Momma got out of the house tonight; let's celebrate!" I'm still the same person at heart, and I'll always be myself, but that night I saw myself growing up and having responsibilities that I'd never had before, and I liked it.

Just because the baby was dominating our lives didn't mean Hank and I didn't need to take a little time for us. Relationships fail because couples forget about the romance. It's so easy to focus on the baby, but you need to find time to have that relationship with the man you fell in love with.

There was a point after the Super Bowl when we got back to Indy that I said to Hank, "Look, I'm starting to feel not loved right now. In the past few weeks, there wasn't one time when we looked at each other and said, 'I love you' or 'You look good today.' "

"I understand what you're saying," he replied. "It's been a while since we really had our time."

So we started having date nights as often as possible—we even tried to take a horse-and-carriage ride around the city, but it was too cold so we cut it short.

I'm fortunate enough to have the freedom to raise Hank Jr. in a loving environment and to spend quality time with his father every now and then. My mom didn't have such luck. She struggled so hard every day to provide for us and still made it to every one of my soccer games.

I'm blessed with the gift of free time, so I'll be on the PTA and go to every play or soccer game or whatever it is that my son is interested in doing. And if he has a teacher who tells him he can't be a marine biologist, I'll be at that school in a heartbeat, ready to kick some ass.

But just because I'm getting a whole new set of responsibilities and will be facing challenges as a mom doesn't mean I will stop living. After all, if you don't go out and continue to explore the world around you, you become like a caged bunny. And as you know by now, I am not, nor will I ever be, a bunny.

My life has been a series of hellos and quick good-byes. As a kid I wanted to make my own rules so I ran away from home.

Then, when I saw an opportunity to better my life, I ran to Hef and the Playboy Mansion.

When I fell in love, I ran right into Hank's arms.

And when I knew I had to put family first, I packed my bags and ran with Hank to Philly, and then to Indy.

I've learned that I don't need to be in such a rush to move on to the next person or place. Life is filled with risks worth taking and new adventures worth running toward, and it's better when you stop running away from something and start running toward new things.

A few months after football season, we moved—as a family— back to Los Angeles. It was my fifth house in less than a year.

Hank and I were glad to be back in the sun and near friends and family and settled (at least for now) in our new home.

Being back in L.A. is amazing, but no matter where we end up or what life throws our way, I'll be happy, as long as Hank and Hank Jr. are by my side. I guess that's what being a mother is all about. I like growing up and I like change, and every day I can't wait to see what happens next.

Hank and I are a perfect team. The day we moved into the L.A. home we had sex three times. We didn't have furniture yet, but we did have a big-ass shower.

I guess some things never change.

Acknowledgments

*P*utting my life down on paper was not easy. And now that it's all said and done, I think I appreciate the people in my life even more than before—which I didn't think was even possible! On that note, I'd like to thank my mom for sticking by me through thick and thin, my grandma for always believing in me, and my brother for always having my back. I'd also like to thank Hank for being the most loving and devoted husband, Hank's parents for being the best in-laws a wife could have, Hef for lifting me up and guiding me on the right path, the Mansion staff for all their hard work over the years, Holly and Bridget for being my girls next door, and Brittany Byars for being my best friend.

Two incredible television shows came out of my years living at the Mansion. I'd like to thank Kevin Burns for producing the best shows ever, Lauren Weinstein and Becca Gullion for putting up with my shit on the show, and to my camera crew for capturing the best (and worst) moments of my life.

Finally, I'd like to thank Emily Westlake, Jen Bergstrom, Louise Burke, Patrick Price, and Michael Nagin from Gallery Books, writer Jon Warech, my literary agent, Dan Strone; my agent Brian; and publicist Kira for hookin' it up.

Without these people, this book would not have been possible.

Jon Warech would also like to thank the team at Gallery Books, master of all agents Kirby Kim, *Girls Next Door* fans/grandparents Joy and Sandy Warech, Katie Warech, Victoria Van Bell, Robert Eth, the Bruce Family, Tracey Heiken, Gena Oppenheim, and the great Gator Nation.